RISE & SHINE

90 Day Devotional for Women, including
Evidence-Based Healing Foods

DEVINA HUGHES COLLIER

Biblical Naturopathic Practitioner, Sclerologist, Iridologist, Certified
Nutrition Consultant, Certified Natural Health Professional.

Published by: Divine Natural Solutions - Private Healthcare Membership Association. P.O. Box 515 Flowery Branch, GA 30542 USA

ISBN-13: 978-0692051214
ISBN-10: 069205121X

Medical Disclaimer: Devina Collier is not a physician or claiming to be a physician. If you have a serious medical condition, seek a physician for proper medical care. The botanicals listed in this book are strictly for reference and educational purposes.

** You may also become a member of her private healthcare membership association and receive naturopathic services. Visit DivineNaturalSolutions.com

DEDICATION

God:	To my Heavenly Father, Jehovah Jireh – my provider Jesus Christ and the Holy Spirit. Thank You for moving mountains.
Tirus:	To my husband - a mighty man of valor. I love you. Thank you for your service in the USA Army and Coast Guard. Thank you for keeping watch, praying, and inspiring me to write.
My 5 Brothers:	Twon, Pumpkin, Vano, Mano, and Fudge. I look at you and see remnants of mom and dad. I see a love that surpasses all understanding.
Ms. Maria Matus. A woman of great compassion:	I never forgot the sacrifices you made for me when I was a teenager. Once, I was sick, you took me to a physician and payed the fee with your own money. Gracias Mama! I am grateful for your family, Josefa, Sara, Bertha, Jennifer and Adolfo. I love you all.
The Readers:	This is the season you've been patiently praying for. Healing belongs to you! May God saturate sweet healing into your every hurt, pain and wound. May you Rise and Shine for greatness!

 To the memory of my beautiful mother, Mrs. Betty Jean Hughes. She was blessed with many God-given talents and gifts. Her father was a World War II USA Navy Veteran. Her mother is a savvy business owner. I am proud to come from mom's DNA. God made us for such a time as this. He never made a mistake. He's intentional! ~ HELLO SWEET VICTORY! ~

One of her many gifts was creativity and art.

Mom's sweet voice was the first voice to wake me in the mornings. She whispered, "RISE AND SHINE." Those words expressed love, joy, hope, greater days and a brighter future. Notice her handwriting – the "y" and "g" resembles the Christian Ichthys (FISH). ♥

Devina H. Collier

CONTENTS

Devina H. Collier

Devina H. Collier

About Devina Renee

Opiate addiction and illness took her mother's young life. The enemy didn't know, however, that God would raise up her only girl child to help the sick heal with only God's natural resources and the Word of God. Devina is not going to allow the enemy to keep people in the dark about how to heal naturally and sufficiently. God hears the prayers of the sick. Devina is led to lead the people into the best health outcome so they can gain strength to do things God called them to do in this life. Just like the walls of Jericho fell. King David used a slingshot and a rock, Devina stands in the gap and teaches how to avoid being destroyed from a lack of knowledge about true healing. *Hosea 4:6 - My people are destroyed for lack of knowledge.*

God called Devina into the healing ministry when she was 12 years old, so when she turned 18, He began preparing her with life-long bible studies, and a traditional and unorthodox education. Today she is the founder of Divine Natural Solutions – a Private Healthcare Membership Association. Her faith is Pentecostal and Bible-believing, and she does not practice any forms of New Age religions.

Devina is an expert with years of combined experience in the traditional medical field, and natural health (alternative medicine and naturopathy). She holds a degree in Doctor of Biblical Naturopathy from Life Training Institute School and Ministry and Seminary.

She is an active practitioner, and teaches live, online Women's Health and Wellness Bible Studies. She published 8 Health and Wellness books in 2016 and is the Alternative Medicine writer for The Christian View TV Talk Show's Online Magazine. They won 2 Awards for Best in Media in 2015 and 2016 and nominated for Rising in Community Excellence Awards in 2017 (RICE Awards). She has been on Atlanta Live TV 57, and also spoke on radio and been interviewed live by women's ministries.

She works with children, teens, adults, and athletes. She utilizes all natural, non-invasive assessment tools to assist her members with their wellness goals. Her education background includes Inner Healing and Deliverance, Cleansing the Temple, Iridology, Sclerology, Detox, Weight Loss, Functional Analysis, Orthomolecular Nutrition, Children's Health, Chemistry of Health, Nutrition and Health, Anatomy and Physiology, Herbal Materia Medica, Nutritional Philosophy, Nutritional Wellness,

Kinesiology, Enzyme Health, Diet and Nutrition, Medical Chemistry, Body Symptoms A-Z, Children's Nutrition and Vaccinations, Teen and Adult Nutrition, Women and Men's Health, Body Systems, and Medical Assisting.

What is Iridology and Sclerology: It's not New Age as some might think it is. There are New Age practitioners that do practice it. Iridology and Sclerology are a science that analyzes eye blood vessels, iris fibers, colors, genetic structure and shapes to reveal a person's health challenges. A camera, Iriscope, or magnifying glass is used to analyze the iris and sclera.

The sclera is the white part of the eye, and it reveals health challenges 6 months to 2 years in advance, while the irises reveal health challenges from birth to current day. How can this be? God didn't hide this science from us. Just like a dermatologist can look at a person's skin and identify a skin disorder, the eyes can reveal organ imbalances with 98% accuracy, including skin challenges. In addition to this, personality traits, gifts and talents are also revealed from birth.

Eyes (irises) have been studied for centuries.
The eyes are extensions of the brain and reveal the blueprints to organ systems' health and vitality. Iridology is the only science that tells

inherent weaknesses. We die from our inherent weaknesses. Disease migrates to our weaknesses. We become toxic laden because we cannot detoxify. Inherent weaknesses tell us where the minerals are needed. – Dr. Jim Jenks.

Iridology is a 2,000-year-old science. It dates to the Chaldeans, according to the German Iridologist, Theodore Kriege. Some of the pioneers of Iridology are Dr. Ignatz von Peczely, Dr. Niles Niljequist, Pastor Felke, Dr. Henry Edward Lane, MD, Dr. Henry Lindlahr, MD, Dr. R. M. McLain, Dr. F. W. Collins, Dr. Haskel Fritzer, Dr. Peter Johannes Thiel, and many more.

<u>What can be revealed:</u> (Iris and Sclera reveal the following:

- Which organs are in greatest need of repair and rebuilding.
- The genetic primary nutritional needs of your body.
- Strong or weak organs, glands and tissues.
- Blood vessel health and restriction.
- Tissue inflammation and where located in the body.
- Hyper or underactive stomach, small intestines or bowel.
- Slow nutrient absorption and how to balance it.

- High-risk tissue areas that may be leading to a disease.
- Sluggish circulation of organ systems, including the brain.
- Lymphatic / Immune / bloodstream congestion (debris, pathogen activity).
- Skin pore blockage or congestion and where located.
- Adrenal suppression and physical or mental fatigue on the body.
- Recuperative ability and the health level of the body.
- Genetic influence on any symptoms present.
- Acidity and alkalinity of the body.
- The quality of nerve force in the body.
- Whether a program or therapy is working or not.
- The "whole" overall health level of the body as a unified structure.

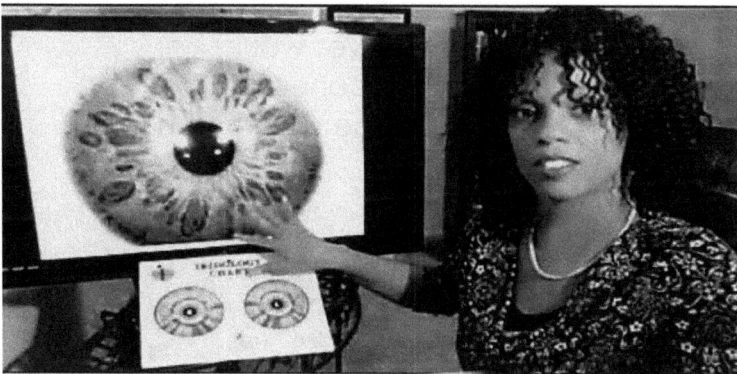

Iridology Chart by Dr. Bernard Jensen and Ellen Tart-Jensen, PhD.

Poem: Momma, I Wish!

By Angela Washington

You're hidden in my heart,
where only God can see.
I wish you were here.
I wish you were with me.
I wish that I could call you
and talk about my day.
I'd share with you some miracles,
and how God made a way.
I may would even cry,
when things got rough,
but I wouldn't cry for long.
Life has made me strong.
I pray through my troubles,
and all life's bad news.
Sometimes I get bruised,
but God will heal my wounds.
I think about you momma.
and how our lives would be.
Although, we cannot touch,
You will always be a part of me.

PART 1: How to Follow This Book?

This book can be used for group Bible Studies
and a Devotional.

There are 2 parts. The 1st part is the Bible Study
and Devotional. The 2nd part is Evidence-Based
Healing Foods.

♥   Enjoy Your Study, Queen! ♥

Day 1: Daughters of the Most High God

(To get good and saturated. Day 1 devotion is longer)

The long, dark night is pierced with light by the loving hand of the Father. And our season of mourning is turned into dancing as the light of Jesus shines through the horizon of our hearts.

If you've ever seen a magnificent sunrise, brilliant with color, and lighting up the horizon, you've had a glimpse of the magnificent beauty that God brings after a long night.

In Bible times, putting on sackcloth was a symbol of intense mourning for the loss of a loved one. The stiff, course material was uncomfortable, reminding the wearer of their intense sorrow. The sackcloth of oppression is that persistent covering of heaviness. But God - our merciful God removes our sackcloth of sickness, sorrow, and oppression. He clothes us with gladness, as sure as He paints the sky at sunrise with radiant, miraculous colors of light.

Through the Lord's mercies, we are not consumed, because His compassions fail not. They are new every morning; great is His faithfulness.

The Lord is my portion," says my soul, Therefore I hope in Him!" - Lamentations 3:22-24

It takes the Lord's strength to break the effects of oppression off the body because oppression is relentless in seeking to dominate our soul. If it can suppress the soul, then it can suppress organs by interfering with their healing processes. Peace and healing can occur when we let go of things we cannot change. Ladies, think of your mental stability when heavy oppression tries to show its face. According to laboratory tests, oppression burns up the body's mineral reserves (electrolytes) and promotes stress and weakness in cells.

When we reject God's word – His knowledge and wisdom to lead us in our lives we are saying to God we don't trust Him to guide us. Heavy oppression can then take legal ground in our lives and affect us wholly. Isaiah 30:12-13 tell us oppression is iniquity. *"Wherefore thus saith the Holy One of Israel, Because ye despise this word, and trust in oppression and perverseness, and stay thereon: Therefore this iniquity shall be to you as a breach ready to fall, swelling out in a high wall, whose breaking cometh suddenly at an instant."*

Be careful not to harbor the effects of oppression in your heart. Just reject it! Give yourself permission to heal. Allow God to break the effects of it from your mind, (soul), body and spirit.

1 Thessalonians 5:23 - And the very God of peace sanctify you wholly; and I pray God your whole spirit and soul and body be preserved blameless unto the coming of our Lord Jesus Christ.

How do you break heavy oppression off you? By commanding it to leave you with your words. I have never seen a war fought in silence. Shout and say each offense by name – if it's a person, for example, say their name. Tell Jesus to remove the oppression from your mind, (soul), body and spirit Then ask Him to forgive you for holding onto it. Then thank Him for removing it. Be advised, you may still go through trials and distresses in life, but the good news is that oppression will not rule you when you ask Jesus to strip it off you.

Psalm 107:13" Then they cried unto the Lord in their trouble, and he saved them out of their distresses." God's word tells us in John 1:5, *"And the light shineth in darkness; and the darkness comprehended it not."* Psalm 30:11 *"You have turned for me my mourning into dancing; You have put off my sackcloth and clothed me with gladness..."*

Though the night seems long, there is joy in the morning. His mercies are new each day. No matter how dark your season, the Father is faithful to cause His Son to rise over your suffering and bring the much-awaited morning.

Get up early one day this week and find a spot to watch the sunrise. Record or draw what you see. Journal about the tender mercies of the Lord and the gladness He places in your heart at that moment.

Prayer and Action Steps:

_____

_____

_____

_____

_____

_____

_____

_____

_____

_____

_____

_____

_____

_____

_____

_____

_____

_____

_____

_____

_____

_____

Devina H. Collier

Body Image
Day 2: A Matter of the Heart

But the Lord said unto Samuel, Look not on his countenance, or on the height of his stature; because I have refused him: for the Lord seeth not as man seeth; for man looketh on the outward appearance, but the Lord looketh on the heart.
1 Samuel 16:7

When God commanded the prophet Samuel to anoint one of Jesse's sons as king of Israel, Samuel thought for sure that the kingship would go to the oldest son Eliab. Because of his prominent stature and appearance, Samuel assumed He would be God's first choice. But the Lord discounted each of Jesse's sons as they passed before the prophet, except for the youngest—David, the shepherd boy. The one that was forgotten and unimportant was the chosen king. He was a man after God's own heart.

Are you a woman after God's own heart? Are you spending more time on your outward appearance than time in worship, prayer, and

Devina H. Collier

Bible study? Don't be fooled by outward appearances. The Lord looks at the heart. Healing occurs from the inside out because the heart is linked to organs, mind (soul), body and spirit.

Action Steps: In column one, write all the positive things about your physical appearance. In the second column, write some positive things about your character (your heart/soul). Which list is longer? Begin to focus first and foremost on matters of the heart. The rest will follow.

Write Your Prayer and Action Steps:

Physical (positives)	Character (positives)

Devina H. Collier

Day 3: Divine Image

So God created man in His own image; in the image of God He created him; male and female He created them.
Genesis 1:27

I can't imagine that the first human beings, Adam and Eve, had any issues with body image. They were created by a personal and loving God who spent time in sweet fellowship with them. He fashioned them in His own image—perfect and complete.

Unfortunately, when sin entered the world, man's view of God was tainted. The enemy lied to them and has been lying to us. He wants nothing more than for us to forget the Divine Image in Whom we were created.

When we look in the mirror and think negative thoughts about ourselves, we are forgetting who we resemble. Remember, we were knitted together by a magnificent Creator and designed to reflect His image!

Devina H. Collier

From whom the whole body fitly joined together and compacted by that which every joint supplieth, according to the effectual working in the measure of every part, maketh increase of the body unto the edifying of itself in love. (Ephesians 4:16)

Let's declare today, that we are daughters of the Most High! Let's praise the Lord for His perfect design and thank Him for creating us to bear His image and walk in sweet fellowship with Him.

Action Steps: Pray and then list 10 of God's divine qualities and know that those same qualities exist in you! See Psalm 145 for help.

Prayer and Action Steps:

_____
_____
_____
_____
_____
_____
_____
_____
_____
_____
_____
_____

Day 4: Marvelous!

I will praise You, for I am fearfully and wonderfully made; marvelous are Your works, and that my soul knows very well.
Psalm 139:14

When God's children are busy praising Him, they don't have much time to complain about body image or something else. Praise the Lord for His goodness. Fill your soul with truths about His marvelous works.

Begin to view yourself as a beautiful woman, confident in the completeness you have in Christ. Reject any words that are contrary to the absolute truth that you are fearfully and wonderfully made.

Action Steps: What physical flaws do you tend to focus on? Write it and then draw a line across it and write "CANCELLED." Repeat to yourself "I am Fearfully and Wonderfully made," as a symbolic act of releasing those self-perceived flaws to the Lord. Tell yourself "I am a magnificent part of God's creation!"

Devina H. Collier

Prayer and Action Steps:

_____

_____

_____

_____

_____

_____

_____

_____

_____

_____

_____

_____

_____

_____

_____

_____

_____

_____

_____

_____

_____

_____

_____

_____

Devina H. Collier

Day 5: Your Body is a Temple

Do you not know that your body is the temple of the Holy Spirit who is in you, whom you have from God, and you are not your own? For you were bought at a price; therefore glorify God in your body and in your spirit, which are God's.
1 Corinthians 6:19-20

Our bodies are temples of the Holy Spirit who lives in us. What an honor! What a privilege! He deserves to receive the highest honor and praise. Once we realize that our bodies are not our own, but dwellings for the Spirit of God, we will no longer waste our energy on fruitless things that gratify the flesh. Our strength should be spent on glorifying Him in every way possible because that will increase our strength.

Ladies, we were bought for a price—the price of Jesus' blood was shed for each of us. Because of His sacrificial purchase, let's make it our goal to live for Him and not ourselves. Let's treat our bodies as the holy temples that they are.

Devina H. Collier

Will you do that today? Will you commit to viewing your body as a temple?

Action Steps: Write out a prayer of commitment to treat your body as the temple of the Holy Spirit. Pray for strength and write action steps you feel you need to take. Ask God to forgive you for the ways in which you have not glorified Him.

Prayer and Action Steps:

_____

_____

_____

_____

_____

_____

_____

_____

_____

_____

_____

_____

_____

_____

_____

_____

_____

_____

          Devina H. Collier

Day 6: What is Your Part?

*For we are his workmanship, created in Christ
Jesus unto good works, which God hath before
ordained that we should walk in them.*
Ephesians 2:10

You are an important and integral part of the
body of Christ. No one else can do exactly what
you were designed to do. He truly has a specific
purpose for your life! However, when we doubt
ourselves and let a negative view of our bodies
get in the way of His purpose, we can easily
become complacent and ineffective.

What specific thing has God prepared for you to
do? What are the gifts and strengths He has
assigned to you? Ask Him to remove any obstacles
that are standing in the way of walking in
obedience to His call on your life. Remember, you
are His workmanship—His masterpiece!

Action Steps: If you don't know what
your God-given strengths are, consider
taking a "strengths" test. Here are a

couple of links that may help you discover your spiritual gifts:

- http://www.lifeway.com/lwc/files/lwcF_MY CS_030526_Spiritual_Gifts_Survey.pdf
- http://buildingchurch.net/g2s-i.htm

Prayer and Action Steps:

_____
_____
_____
_____
_____
_____
_____
_____
_____
_____
_____
_____
_____
_____
_____
_____
_____
_____
_____
_____

Self-Discipline
Day 7: What Freedom Means

You, my brothers and sisters, were called to be free. But do not use your freedom to indulge the flesh; rather, serve one another humbly in love.
Galatians 5:13

As Christians, we often use the phrase, "I've been set free." But what do we really mean by that? Have we been set free to do whatever we want, whenever we want? Of course not!

Ladies, we were set free by the blood of Jesus Christ and set apart for His glory. We were called to the highest levels of holiness—to walk according to the Spirit and not the flesh. (Galatians 5:16)

In a world that promotes instant gratification, it is tempting to indulge in things that satisfy our cravings. But ladies, let's not mistake our freedom in Christ to self-indulge, but serve others in love. By taking the focus off ourselves, we will be less tempted to give in to our own desires. Begin to view freedom as an opportunity to serve, not to be served. Stand fast in the freedom for which Christ made you free! (Galatians 5:1)

Action Steps: What are your biggest temptations? What areas of self-indulgence do you need the most help? Take some time to examine your life and start eliminating things that cause you to stumble.

Prayer and Action Steps:

_____
_____
_____
_____
_____
_____
_____
_____
_____
_____
_____
_____
_____
_____
_____
_____
_____
_____
_____
_____

Devina H. Collier

Devina H. Collier

Day 8: Everything You Need

*According as his divine power hath given unto us
all things that pertain unto life and godliness,
through the knowledge of him that hath
called us to glory and virtue.*
2 Peter 1:3

It's easy to confuse self-discipline with self-reliance. We forget that it is only by God's divine power that we are truly able to live a life of holiness. Self-reliance will always fail us, at some point. God's desire is that we would fully depend on Him in every area of life.

The Bible tells us, in 2 Peter, that we have *everything we need* pertaining to life and godliness, through His divine power and the knowledge of Him who called us. Think about that for a minute. We have everything we need, ladies! Not one thing is lacking! Our generous God has provided the way for us. We don't have to wonder how we are going to achieve our goals. We just need to focus on doing His will according to His glory and virtue. Amen. Glory to His name.

Devina H. Collier

Action Steps: write out 2 Peter 1:3. Any time you feel like you don't have what it takes to succeed, speak this truth aloud and know you already have everything you need to be a successful woman of God. Write what you need now, and what you already have – include your health. If you need to make adjustments in your life. Include some action steps as well.

Prayer and Action Steps:

_____

_____

_____

_____

_____

_____

_____

_____

_____

_____

_____

_____

_____

_____

_____

_____

_____

_____

Rise and Shine

Devina H. Collier

Day 9: Is It Beneficial?

*All things are lawful unto me, but all things are
not expedient: all things are lawful for me, but I
will not be brought under the power of any.*
1 Corinthians 6:12

To feel powerless under the sway of temptation is
a terrible feeling. But sometimes, we allow habits
to form, thinking they are harmless, when really,
they are not beneficial to us at all. We must be
discerning in what we allow in our lives, even if it
seems harmless on the surface.

Part of being self-disciplined is being able to
recognize what helps us thrive, and what hinders
us from being our best selves. What "permissible"
things in your life are unfruitful things that you
should get rid of? What kind of power do those
things have over you?

Action Steps: Commit to discarding ONE
HABIT this week that may be permissible,
but not beneficial. Confide in a friend for
prayer and accountability also.

Devina H. Collier

Prayer and Action Steps:

_____

_____

_____

_____

_____

_____

_____

_____

_____

_____

_____

_____

_____

_____

_____

_____

_____

_____

_____

_____

_____

_____

_____

_____

_____

_____

_____

_____

Devina H. Collier

Day 10: Strong Tower

He that hath no rule over his own spirit is like a
city that is broken down, and without walls.
Proverbs 25:28

No one likes to feel weak, especially to sin. When we allow our flesh to get out of control, we are like crumbling walls ready to collapse. But remember, self-control is a fruit of the Holy Spirit. It is He who strengthens us to be like fortified walls that cannot fall.

Stand strong in the Lord today and know that you don't have to muster your own strength to resist sin. You need only to declare that He is a mighty fortress, able to help you withstand every temptation and every circumstance. The Name of the Lord is a strong tower; the righteous run to it and are safe. (Proverbs 18:10)

Action Steps: Find an image of a stone wall and use it as a screen saver. Every time you see it, remember that you are a woman of strength, fortified by the Holy Spirit of God! Now command that weakness to leave you and tell Jesus to strip it off your mind (soul), body and spirit. Try this free photo site: www.pixabay.com

Prayer and Action Steps:

_____
_____
_____
_____
_____
_____
_____
_____
_____
_____
_____
_____
_____
_____
_____
_____
_____
_____
_____
_____
_____
_____

Day 11: Run with Certainty

I therefore so run, not as uncertainly; so fight I, not as one that beateth the air: But I keep under my body, and bring it into subjection...
1 Corinthians 9:26-27

To bring something into subjection means to bring it under authority. We don't eat right and exercise because we are subject to man, but to our Ultimate Authority—God. It's by Him, for Him, and because of Him that we are running this race at all. And this race is not a sprint, my sisters, but a marathon. Truly, it does take determination and perseverance to finish well.

Why are you running? For what are you striving? Is it to please man or God? Ladies, let's run with certainty and purpose, bringing our flesh into subjection under the divine authority of God. Let's fight this good fight with intentionality!

Action Steps: Take a walk, run, or hike today and write about how you are bringing your body into subjection, not to man, but to God.

Prayer and Action Steps:

_____
_____
_____
_____
_____
_____
_____
_____
_____
_____
_____
_____
_____
_____
_____
_____
_____
_____
_____
_____
_____
_____
_____
_____
_____
_____

Devina H. Collier

Anxiety
Day 12: A Spirit of Power

For God hath not given us the spirit of fear; but of power, and of love, and of a sound mind.
2 Timothy 1:7

What causes fear within us? Think about that for a moment. Fear comes when we feel *powerless* over our circumstances. When we sense that something is out of our control, we give in to fear. However, no circumstance on earth can override our God-given spirit of power, love, and a sound mind. The Lord has empowered us with sober minds of reason, intelligence, and clarity. He has given us beating hearts of fervent love. And He has instilled in us spirits of power fueled by His Holy Spirit.

When adversity comes and threatens to leave us feeling helpless, we can at once rebuke that spirit of fear. Then, we can proclaim our God-given spirit of power over every situation.

Devina H. Collier

Action Steps: What brings you the most fear? What leaves you feeling helpless? Speak your fears aloud and give yourself permission to face them head-on. Then, rebuke them in the mighty name of Jesus!

Prayer and Action Steps:

_____

_____

_____

_____

_____

_____

_____

_____

_____

_____

_____

_____

_____

_____

_____

_____

_____

_____

_____

_____

_____

_____

        Devina H. Collier

Day 13: Perfect Peace

Peace I leave with you, my peace I give unto you: not as the world giveth, give I unto you. Let not your heart be troubled, neither let it be afraid.
John 14:27

The peace Jesus gives, to every believer, is not the superficial peace that the world offers. The world's shallow promises of happiness cannot take the place of true peace. Food, alcohol, spending, and other instant gratifications are temporary comforts, but they can never give us the fulfillment we long for. Only Jesus provides His perfect peace that supersedes anything this world has to offer.

When Jesus said, "Let not your heart be troubled," He was reminding us that we have the *choice* to prevent anxious thoughts from lingering in our minds. He gave us His Spirit to remind us of everything He taught and everything we ought to be thinking about instead. (John 14:26)

What are you dwelling on today? What worldly comforts are you seeking to bring you peace?

Devina H. Collier

Remember, only Jesus is our *perfect peace*.

Action Steps: Write an acrostic poem for the word P-E-A-C-E. For each letter, write a Biblical truth about the peace and comfort the Lord gives. Look to the Psalms for ideas.

Prayer and Action Steps:

P	
E	
A	
C	
E	

Day 14: True Delight

*In the multitude of my anxieties within me, Your
comforts delight my soul.*
Psalm 94:19

Whatever brings your soul delight and whatever
brings a smile to your face—those are precious
gifts from God. His comforts, in the midst of our
anxieties, are limitless. However, in our emotional
stress, we easily miss those wonderful gifts of joy.

Having true joy is not to be confused with being
happy. Happiness is a fleeting emotion that
comes and goes, depending on the ups and
downs of life. Godly joy, however, is a permanent
delight penetrating our souls—no matter what life
brings.

In the multitude of your anxieties, ask God for His
inexplicable joy. He will give it! He longs to delight
your soul. For His joy is your strength. Nehemiah
8:10

Devina H. Collier

Action Steps: What blessings bring you true joy? Take time to thank God for those precious gifts today. Write "thank you" to the Lord as a reminder of His blessings, and a few action steps you can take to naturally reduce your anxiety.

Prayer and Action Steps:

_____

_____

_____

_____

_____

_____

_____

_____

_____

_____

_____

_____

_____

_____

_____

_____

_____

_____

_____

_____

_____

Day 15: His Righteous Right Hand

Fear thou not; for I am with thee: be not dismayed; for I am thy God: I will strengthen thee; yea, I will help thee; yea, I will uphold thee with the right hand of my righteousness.
Isaiah 41:10

I heard a Pastor once say, that our feelings can change like the shifting of the wind. Unpredictable and unreliable, our feelings cannot be trusted to guide us through the journey of life. Faith, on the other hand, is based on the certainty we have in Christ—the certainty of His divine presence to strengthen and guide us. Even when we cannot *feel* the presence of the Lord, we can be assured that He is there.

When the Bible tells us that God upholds us with His righteous, right hand, it means that we are upheld by Jesus Himself. For the Son is seated at the right hand of the Father and is our Righteous Redeemer. (Colossians 3:1)

Devina H. Collier

Action Steps: Read Hebrews chapter 11. Journal about the specific ways the patriarchs of faith led by example. Ask God to strengthen you to walk in faith instead of feelings. Write how you will trust God to guide you through life.

Prayer and Action Steps:

_____

_____

_____

_____

_____

_____

_____

_____

_____

_____

_____

_____

_____

_____

_____

_____

_____

_____

_____

_____

_____

_____

_____

Day 16: He Got You!

Therefore humble yourselves under the mighty hand of God, that He may exalt you in due time, casting all your cares upon Him, for He cares for you.
1 Peter 5:6-7

When anxious thoughts consume us, it's hard to think of anything else. We may find ourselves fretting and agitated, unable to calm down. But it's at these times, when we desperately need to go to our prayer closets and humble ourselves under the mighty hand of God.

He is the only One who can take what concerns us and work it out for our good. Even when we don't know what to pray, it's OK. He already knows every anxious thought we have. The regular practice of humbling ourselves in His presence is the best way to deal with anxiety. Trust that He will lift you up—at just the right time and in just the right way. Will you cast your cares upon Him today?

Action Steps: Find a "prayer closet" somewhere in your house, where you can be alone with the Lord. Write your cares as they come and any action steps you need to take. Then, as you spend time in prayer, cross your cares off the list as He delivers you.

Prayer and Action Steps:

_____
_____
_____
_____
_____
_____
_____
_____
_____
_____
_____
_____
_____
_____
_____
_____
_____
_____
_____
_____
_____

Depression
Day 17: His Lavish Love

Now hope does not disappoint, because the love of God has been poured out in our hearts by the Holy Spirit who was given to us.
Romans 5:5

It's true that life is full of many disappointments. Things we hope for don't come. People we count on let us down. And aspirations we have don't always happen. However, it's what we do with those disappointments that either leads us to a renewed sense of purpose, or to a place of defeat.

Dear sisters, there is always hope! No matter how bleak the situation might seem, hope does not disappoint. Even if everything around us fails our God will never fail. His love alone is enough to overcome any and every disappointment.

Sometimes, I think we take the Lord's love for granted. We forget just how lavish He really is. The Scriptures say that His love has been *poured out* in our hearts. That shows an abundant flow that fills

Devina H. Collier

us to overflowing! Nothing on this earth can overshadow the Lord's amazing love.

Action Steps: Read the following verses that describe God's incredible love. Journal your thoughts and any action steps that you would like to take. Psalm 86:15, Jeremiah 31:3, Zephaniah 3:17, Romans 5:8, Ephesians 2:4-5, 1 John 3:1

Prayer and Action Steps:

_____

_____

_____

_____

_____

_____

_____

_____

_____

_____

_____

_____

_____

_____

_____

_____

_____

_____

_____

_____

Day 18: Capturing Negative Thoughts

Finally, brethren, whatsoever things are true, whatsoever things are honest, whatsoever things are just, whatsoever things are pure, whatsoever things are lovely, whatsoever things are of good report; if there be any virtue, and if there be any praise, think on these things.
Philippians 4:8

The continuous cycle of thoughts in our minds can resemble a hamster wheel, spinning around and around, but never going anywhere. The longer we stay on the "hamster wheel," the harder it is to step off.

2 Corinthians 10:5 says that we are to "cast down imaginations, and every high thing that exalteth itself against the knowledge of God, and bring into captivity every thought to the obedience of Christ."

Ladies, this means we are not supposed to entertain negative thinking. We have the choice and the obligation to bring into captivity every thought. Practically, this means that when unworthy things first enter our minds, we need to capture them and release them to the Lord. We should, in essence, step immediately off the "hamster wheel."

What consumes your mind? Are they negative thoughts that spiral out of control? Or, are they thoughts of honesty, purity, and loveliness?

Action Steps: Take a walk outside today and make a mental list of all the praiseworthy things you see. Trees, birds, fresh air, sunshine, kids playing... all things that we can praise our Heavenly Father for.

Prayer and Action Steps:

_____

_____

_____

_____

_____

_____

_____

_____

_____

_____

_____

_____

_____

Devina H. Collier

Day 19: Praise in the Darkness

Why are you cast down, O my soul? And why are you disquieted within me? Hope in God; for I shall yet praise Him, the help of my countenance and my God.
Psalm 42:11

In Psalm 42, the sons of Korah sing a song of remembrance and desperate longing for the Living God. It's as if they are remembering better times, when there was joy in the house of the Lord. Their lament speaks of tears and mourning, oppression and reproach. It seemed to be a dark and depressing time in history.

But right in the middle of this heartrending Psalm, we read... *"The Lord will command His lovingkindness in the daytime, and in the night His song shall be with me—a prayer to the God of my life." (vs. 8)*

What encouragement for us, sisters! To know that no matter how dark our circumstances, the Lord commands His lovingkindness to surround us. Day and night, He is with us.

Devina H. Collier

Action Steps: When your soul is downcast, sing a song of praise. Put together a playlist of your favorite worship songs and turn on the music every time you feel disquieted in your soul. List the songs you picked for the action steps.

Prayer and Action Steps:

_____

_____

_____

_____

_____

_____

_____

_____

_____

_____

_____

_____

_____

_____

_____

_____

_____

_____

_____

_____

_____

_____

Day 20: Your Testimony

I waited patiently for the Lord; and He inclined to me, and heard my cry. He also brought me up out of a horrible pit, out of the miry clay, and set my feet upon a rock, and established my steps. He has put a new song in my mouth—praise to our God…
Psalm 40:1-3

Have you, by your own strength, made a name for yourself? Do you feel successful because you have worked hard to be where you are today? I ask these questions to challenge you to look at the One who made things possible for you. All of us work hard at the tasks we've been given, and hopefully, we are thriving in the call of God on our lives. However, let us never forget the One Who establishes our steps. Let us never forget the place from which He has delivered us.

It's easy to think that we are self-made, and our own strength got us to where we are today. Sometimes we forget why we have the abilities and success we have. Ladies, before you were born, God gave you natural talents and gifts that are to be used to bless your life, but also to bless the body of Christ (His church).

Our heavenly Father is the One who has set our feet upon the Rock—Jesus Christ. He is the One who has secured our path and given us direction in the way we should go. He has blessed us with every achievement and every success.

Action Steps: Recall your life before Christ. What horrible pit did He deliver you from? Consider writing your salvation story as a testimony to others. Someone out there needs to hear your story for His glory!

Prayer and Action Steps:

_____

_____

_____

_____

_____

_____

_____

_____

_____

_____

_____

_____

_____

_____

Devina H. Collier

Day 21: Leap Over a Wall

*For Thou art my lamp, O Lord: and the
Lord will lighten my darkness. For by
Thee I have run through a troop: by my
God have I leaped over a wall.*
2 Samuel 22:29-30

Mighty and miraculous things have been done by the empowerment of the Holy Spirit. The entire nation of Israel was led out of Egypt through the midst of the sea. The walls of Jericho came down with the sound of trumpets and a great shout. Lion's mouths were closed when Daniel was thrown into their den for being faithful to God.

What mighty and miraculous thing are you counting on today? Do you believe? Are you trusting that by the lamp of the Lord you will run through an army of adversity and leap over every wall of opposition?

Action Steps: Challenge yourself to do something courageous this week. Sign up for a 5k in your area, volunteer at your local homeless shelter, or start a neighborhood walking group. Whatever God is pressing on your heart, let go of fear and move forward in victory.

Prayer and Action Steps:

_____
_____
_____
_____
_____
_____
_____
_____
_____
_____
_____
_____
_____
_____
_____
_____
_____
_____
_____
_____
_____
_____

Devina H. Collier

Worry
Day 22: Seek First His Kingdom

*Therefore I say unto you, take no
thought For your life, what ye shall eat, or what
ye shall drink; nor yet for your body, what ye
shall put on. Is not the life more than meat,
and the body than raiment?*
Matthew 6:25

Have you ever stopped to think about the ordinary things we take for granted? We turn a knob and instantly have hot water for bathing. Our closets are overflowing with clothes. We open our refrigerators to reveal an abundance of food. Yet, our focus seems to be fixed on our material needs and the wanting thereof. We spend a lot of time worrying about food, clothing, earthly comforts, and troubles.

When Jesus said, *"Take no thought for your life, what you will eat, drink, or wear,"* He wasn't saying those things aren't important. He was encouraging us to *seek first His kingdom and His righteousness.* Then, all our needs would be met as well. (Matthew 6:33)

Devina H. Collier

Ladies, the Lord knows just what we need for this life. He is Jehovah-Jireh—our Provider.

Action Steps: Take inventory of your food, clothing, and material goods. Consider donating a portion of them to your local homeless shelter. Let's get our focus off our belongings and onto Jesus!

Prayer and Action Steps:

_____
_____
_____
_____
_____
_____
_____
_____
_____
_____
_____
_____
_____
_____
_____
_____
_____
_____
_____
_____

Devina H. Collier

Day 23: Prepare for Rest

I will both lay me down in peace, and sleep:
for thou, Lord, only makest me dwell in safety.
Psalm 4:8

Have you ever had one of those nights where you were physically exhausted, but your mind was too restless to sleep? The worries of the day spin around like an old record that is stuck playing the same part over and over.

When we are under a lot of emotional stress, our bodies react in different ways. One major issue that may arise is insomnia. However, poor sleep can lead to even more physical problems down the road. Good sleep is an important part of ultimate health.

Settling down our minds, as we prepare for bed, is just as important as brushing our teeth. Listening to praise music, or reading the Psalms, are ways to filter out the stress of the day and relax our minds.

How do you prepare for bed? Are you in the habit of watching television or scrolling through your phone? Do you have trouble getting your mind to relax?

Action Steps: For one week, make it a priority to read through or listen to one chapter of the Psalms before bed. Allow God's Word to replace the worries of the day and prepare your mind for rest.

Prayer and Action Steps:

_____

_____

_____

_____

_____

_____

_____

_____

_____

_____

_____

_____

_____

_____

_____

_____

_____

_____

_____

_____

_____

 Devina H. Collier

Day 24: Marvelous Promises

Bless the Lord, O my soul, and forget not all his benefits: who forgiveth all thine iniquities; who healeth all thy diseases; who redeemeth thy life from destruction; who crowneth thee with lovingkindness and tender mercies; who satisfieth thy mouth with good things; so that thy youth is renewed like the eagle's.
Psalm 103:2-5

Worry has a way of causing us to jump from one thought to another, until we forget what we were worried about in the first place. Even though there are legitimate things to be concerned about, it's easy to allow those concerns to grow into an all-consuming cloud of fretfulness.

Psalm 103 lists five powerful promises of God. The Psalm declares that the Lord will *forgive, heal, redeem, crown, and satisfy* us, so that our youth is renewed like the eagle's. Now, ladies, that's encouraging.

The Lord's incredible mercies far outshine any worries we may have. Let's remember these beautiful promises the next time worries hovers like a dark cloud.

Action Steps: Write out the five promises from Psalm 103:2-5. Carry them with you and proclaim them when worry strikes. For even more encouragement, read all of Psalm 103 and write down the other beautiful attributes that are mentioned.

Prayer and Action Steps:

_____

_____

_____

_____

_____

_____

_____

_____

_____

_____

_____

_____

_____

_____

_____

_____

_____

_____

_____

_____

Day 25: Words of the Holy Spirit

"Now when they bring you to the synagogues and magistrates and authorities, do not worry about how or what you should answer, or what you should say. For the Holy Spirit will teach you in that very hour what you ought to say."
Luke 12:11-12

Have you ever been faced with a dreaded confrontation? Even as Christians, we will, on occasion, need to say some hard things to people. God may ask us to stand up for what we believe. He may call us to speak truth into someone's life.

During these times, there is no need to worry about what we are going to say. We can rely on the Holy Spirit to give us the exact words at the very hour we are to speak them. Our job is to pray for wisdom, and to spend time in God's Word, preparing our hearts to receive what the Spirit has for us.

Are you fretting about speaking to someone in your life? A boss, a family member, a friend? Trust that God will give you the right words at the right time. Just remember to approach everyone in a spirit of love and rely on the Lord to direct the conversation.

Action Steps: Instead of rehearsing what you are going to say to someone, go to your prayer closet and pray over the situation. Listen intently to words of wisdom and thank God for preparing the way.

Prayer and Action Steps:

_____
_____
_____
_____
_____
_____
_____
_____
_____
_____
_____
_____
_____
_____
_____
_____
_____
_____

Devina H. Collier

Day 26: Choose whom You Will Serve

Now therefore fear the Lord, and serve him in sincerity and in truth: and put away the gods which your fathers served on the other side of the flood, and in Egypt; and serve ye the Lord. And if it seem evil unto you to serve the Lord, choose you this day whom ye will serve; whether the gods which your fathers served that were on the other side of the flood, or the gods of the Amorites, in whose land ye dwell: but as for me and my house, we will serve the Lord.
Joshua 24:14-15

What does it mean to serve the Lord? That phrase is often quoted within Christian circles, but what does it really mean to *serve* our God and Savior?

In the time of Joshua, after the Lord had led the Israelites into the land He had promised, the people were required to choose whom they would serve. The Lord spoke through Joshua and challenged them to either follow the gods of their forefathers or devote themselves wholly to the One True God.

Devina H. Collier

The Israelites promised to serve the Lord, so Joshua commanded, *"Now therefore put away the strange gods which are among you and incline your heart unto the Lord God of Israel."* (Joshua 24:23)

My sisters, what words of wisdom those are for us! When we choose to serve the Lord, we "put away" worldly lusts and strongholds.

Are we making ourselves useful to the service of God? Are we living in obedience to Him? Or, are we chasing after the "gods" around us? The definition of "serve," is *to be useful, to render active service, or to render obedience.*

Action Steps: Today, think about how you spend your time. Are most hours of the day spent serving your habits, strongholds, or worldly passions? Or, are you rendering yourself useful to God? Write a prayer of renewed commitment to offer yourselves as living sacrifices. Include the words, "As for me and my house, we will serve the Lord," then write what that is and the steps to take

Prayer and Action Steps:

_____

_____

_____

Finances
Day 27: Give First

*Give, and it will be given to you: good
measure, pressed down, shaken together,
and running over will be put into your bosom.
For with the same measure that you use, it
will be measured back to you.*
Luke 6:38

Of all the issues women have, financial struggles
are at the top of the list. We work hard to make
ends meet, but sometimes it becomes
overwhelming to keep count of every penny.

Giving helps spread the gospel of Jesus Christ
around the globe. It is also used to help set the
captives free when ministries purchase resources
to help community causes. *"And whatsoever ye
do, do it heartily, as to the Lord, and not unto men;
Knowing that of the Lord ye shall receive the
reward of the inheritance: for ye serve the Lord
Christ."* (Colossians 3:23-24)

One of the temptations we face during financial
hardship is the resistance to give. Tithings and

Devina H. Collier

offerings become the first things we cut from our budget when things get tough. But ladies, the Lord promise that when we give, we will be mightily blessed. In fact, tithing is mentioned in Malachi 3:10 as an invitation to test God. Did you know that?

Bring the whole tithe into the storehouse, that there may be food in my house. "Test me in this," says the Lord Almighty, "and see if I will not throw open the floodgates of heaven and pour out so much blessing that there will not be room enough to store it."

Give, and it will be given to you, running over and measured back to you. His Word does not lie. We can fully trust the Lord to keep His promises. Don't let fear hold you back from giving what is in your heart to give. Remember, this isn't a legalistic command, but a loving promise.

Action Steps: If you have been reluctant to tithe, confess it to God and know that He is faithful and just to forgive. 1 John 1:9 Then, commit to setting aside the first fruits of your income to give as an offering. Record the blessings as they come flooding in! In your action steps, make a note of what you gave for.

Prayer and Action Steps:

Rise and Shine

_____

_____

_____

_____

_____

_____

_____

_____

_____

_____

_____

_____

_____

_____

_____

_____

_____

_____

_____

_____

_____

_____

_____

_____

_____

_____

_____

_____

_____

_____

Day 28: What Will You Take with You?

For the love of money is a root of all kinds of evil, for which some have strayed from the faith in their greediness, and pierced themselves through with many sorrows.
1 Timothy 6:10

You've heard that money, in and of itself, isn't evil, but the *love* of money is. The Bible warns that people have gone astray because of greed and have pierced themselves with many sorrows.

Ladies, the great deception is that money will bring contentment and happiness. The striving for wealth can entice even the most devoted of Christians. But chasing after riches are a dangerous pursuit. *"For what shall it profit a man, if he shall gain the whole world, and lose his own soul?"* (Mark 8:36)

In the end, we will take nothing with us. Every earthly treasure will be left behind. Let's stop running after monetary gain and start running toward our heavenly reward.

Devina H. Collier

"Lay not up for yourselves treasures upon earth, where moth and rust doth corrupt, and where thieves break through and steal: But lay up for yourselves treasures in heaven, where neither moth nor rust doth corrupt, and where thieves do not break through nor steal: For where your treasure is, there will your heart be also." (Matthew 6:19-21)

Action Steps: How do you view money? Is it constantly on your mind? Try this exercise: Make a list of everything you could ever want (houses, vacations, cars, etc.) Now, circle the things you will take with you to heaven. How many did you circle?

Next, make a list of your heavenly rewards such as perfect peace, true joy, and eternity with Jesus. Circle those things as reminders.

Prayer and Action Steps:

_____

_____

_____

_____

_____

_____

_____

_____

Day 29: Contentment

*Let your conduct be without covetousness; be
content with such things as you have.*
Hebrews 13:5

There is something remarkable about
contentment for sure. Because we live in a world
where nothing is ever enough. It is an amazing
quality to be content with what we have.

You've heard the phrase, "Keeping up with the
Joneses." That phrase was based on a popular
comic strip that was first printed in the New York
Globe in 1913. It was used as a figure of speech to
indicate striving to keep up with a neighbor's
income or social standing.

But the Bible says to let our conduct be without
covetousness. Ladies, we need to be very careful
about comparing our lives to others. When our
friends or neighbors are blessed with material
things, we should rejoice with them, not be jealous
or covetous, because truly there is peace when
we don't covet.

Devina H. Collier

Look around and note the abundant blessings you have been given. Thank God for your life and avoid the temptation to covet someone else's lifestyle.

Action Steps: Write the word "contentment" Then write what God has blessed you with. Let that word become a prominent reminder to be content with what you have.

Prayer and Action Steps:

_____
_____
_____
_____
_____
_____
_____
_____
_____
_____
_____
_____
_____
_____
_____
_____
_____
_____

Devina H. Collier

Rise and Shine

Day 30: The Stronghold of Money

When Delilah saw that he had told her all his heart, she sent and called for the lords of the Philistines, saying, "Come up once more, for he has told me all his heart." So the lords of the Philistines came up to her and brought the money in their hand.
Judges 16:18

For eleven hundred pieces of silver, Delilah was willing to deceive Samson—the man who loved her. Enticed by money, she tricked him into revealing the source of his strength. Her deception didn't just fill her pockets with silver. It eventually led to Samson's death.

Money has a way of convincing us to do less than honorable things. Greed, dishonesty, and selfish gain are a few of its alluring temptations. These are things we should guard against.

The thing is, ladies, God knows our hearts when it comes to money—whether we are handling it with integrity or not. If greed is a struggle, it would be wise to confess it to the Lord and share it with

 Devina H. Collier

your prayer circle so that they can pray for deliverance – but most importantly, tell Jesus to strip it off your soul and body. Shout!

Action Steps: If money has an unhealthy grip on you, consider calling a trusted financial advisor to walk you through the steps of saving, investing, and tithing. It may be just what you need to bring your finances into the proper focus.

Prayer and Action Steps:

_____
_____
_____
_____
_____
_____
_____
_____
_____
_____
_____
_____
_____
_____
_____
_____
_____
_____

Day 31: Diligence

*The plans of the diligent lead surely
to plenty, But those of everyone who
is hasty, surely to poverty.*
Proverbs 21:5

Bit-by-faithful-bit, is a good way to build wealth and invest money properly. It certainly isn't the most popular way to do things, given we live in a society of instant gratification, but it is the *diligent* way of doing things.

The Proverbs teach us that diligent plans lead to plenty, but hastiness leads to poverty. "Get rich quick schemes" are exactly what they describe—schemes.

When we have a healthy mindset about our finances, we can look at the big picture. We have the wisdom to pay our bills on time, give our first fruits to the Lord, and save appropriately. Having a Biblical understanding of money allows us to rest securely in God's provision instead of hastily striving to make a quick dollar.

 Devina H. Collier

Diligence is a sign of strength, not only when it comes to finances, but in our health as well. Bit-by-faithful-bit should become our mindset as we build every good thing in our lives.

Action Steps: What are some small steps you can take to begin handling money wisely? What is one thing you can implement? Remember, it's all about taking small, diligent steps that lead to big success.

Prayer and Action Steps:

_____
_____
_____
_____
_____
_____
_____
_____
_____
_____
_____
_____
_____
_____
_____
_____
_____
_____

Devina H. Collier

Forgiveness
Day 32: Reconciliation

*He that covereth a transgression seeketh love;
but he that repeateth a matter
separateth very friends.*
Proverbs 17:9

Did you know that genuine forgiveness can take place without ever reconciling with the other person? There seems to be a misconception that forgiveness always leads to reuniting with the one who offended us. Although we are commanded to forgive, we aren't necessarily expected to continue in the relationship. Some situations will demand that we go our separate ways—and that's OK.

The heart of the matter is love. We "covereth over" a transgression by the love of God. We may not *feel* loving towards the person who wronged us, but we allow the Holy Spirit to flow through us and make a way for forgiveness. The consequence of the offense might be the separation of close friends, but there can still be genuine forgiveness from the heart.

 Devina H. Collier

How difficult is it for you to forgive? Have you assumed that forgiveness always includes reconciliation?

Consider emailing or writing a letter to someone who has wronged you. Offer genuine forgiveness out of the love God has poured into your heart. Release that person and their offense completely to the Lord.

Prayer and Action Steps:

_____

_____

_____

_____

_____

_____

_____

_____

_____

_____

_____

_____

_____

_____

_____

_____

_____

_____

Day 33: A New Thing

Do not remember the former things, nor consider the things of old. Behold, I will do a new thing, now it shall spring forth; shall you not know it?
Isaiah 43:18-19

We sure can be forgetful, can't we ladies? Dozens of things on our agendas make it easy to forget appointments and other details. But when it comes to people who've hurt us, our memories are as sharp as a tack. We remember every detail!

We may not be able to shake the memory of how we were hurt, but the Bible encourages us not to keep a record of wrongs. (1 Corinthians 13:5 NIV) And even though the mere thought of that person can bring back feelings of betrayal, the Word of God has a beautiful declaration for us…

Do not remember the former things, Nor consider the things of old. Behold, I will do a new thing, Now it shall spring forth; Shall you not know it? I will even make a road in the wilderness And rivers in the desert. (Isaiah 43:18-19)

Devina H. Collier

Those words, meant for the nation of Israel, have great implications for us as well. For the Lord knows that dwelling on the past holds us back from moving forward in victory. Clinging to former hurts keeps us from taking hold of the beautiful things to come. *"Behold, I will do a new thing..."*

Do you believe that today? Do you believe that God can do a new thing in your life? Don't hold on to resentments any longer. Erase every record of wrongs and replace them with the new things God is doing in your life.

Close the door the former things. Look forward to new things. Write the things that you have been dwelling on. Then draw a line through it and write God's word "Behold, I will do a new thing!"

Prayer and Action Steps:

_____
_____
_____
_____
_____
_____
_____
_____
_____
_____

Devina H. Collier

Rise and Shine

Day 34: Times of Refreshment

The Lord is my shepherd; I shall not want. He
makes me to lie down in green pastures; He
leads me beside the still waters. He restores my
soul; He leads me in the paths of righteousness
For His name's sake.
Psalm 23:1-3

At times our souls need restoring, the same way
our organs need refreshing. Unrepentant sins can
certainly block that blessing, but God desires to
refresh us in every aspect of life. Consistent times
of worship, prayer, and Bible study brings us back
to our centeredness in Christ. When we chronically
neglect our spiritual nourishment, we put ourselves
at risk of a disconnect that can lead to all kinds of
sins.

*Repent therefore and be converted, that your sins
may be blotted out, so that times of refreshing
may come from the presence of the Lord. (Acts
3:19)*

Truly, part of our spiritual refreshment involves
repentance. When we confess, we are purging

Devina H. Collier

the things that don't belong. When we fail to confess, and accept God's forgiveness for our sins, we are opening a doorway to illness. Ladies, our spiritual health is vital to our physical health as well.

How will you allow the Lord to refresh you today?

Take a spiritual vacation by scheduling one full day to pray and fast from something (an activity, food, TV, or social media). Ask the Lord to refresh your spirit and bring you back to your centeredness in Christ.

Prayer and Action Steps:

_____

_____

_____

_____

_____

_____

_____

_____

_____

_____

_____

_____

_____

                                    Devina H. Collier

Day 35: Forbearance

Or do you despise the riches of His goodness, forbearance, and longsuffering, not knowing that the goodness of God leads you to repentance?
Romans 2:4

There's a beautiful verse, in Romans chapter 2, that reminds us of God's lovingkindness leading us to repentance. It is contrary to the worldly belief that God is a harsh judge, just waiting for us to mess up. In His forbearance, He is patient and kind, giving us every opportunity to repent.

If our loving Creator treats us with such grace, shouldn't we also treat others the same way? Are you holding onto a grudge or maintaining a heart of un-forgiveness?

My sisters, remember, that holding onto un-forgiveness only hurts us. Mentally, physically, and spiritually, resentment zaps the life of our organs, including stealing the joy of our soul and spirit.

After Jesus encouraged the disciples to forgive "seventy times seven," they asked Him to "increase their faith." Let that be our prayer today... "Lord, increase our faith!"

Take heed to yourselves. If your brother sins against you, rebuke him; and if he repents, forgive him. And if he sins against you seven times in a day, and seven times in a day returns to you, saying, 'I repent,' you shall forgive him. (Luke 17:3-4)

Sisters, how quick are you to forgive? How much "forbearance" do you have toward others?

Today, write the number **490** as a reminder to forgive "seventy times seven." Let God's kindness be your inspiration. Then pray, "Lord, increase my faith!"

Prayer and Forgiving Yourself and Others – For example: self-hatred, self-denial, not forgiving yourself and or others for misstates, hurts, and trauma.

_____
_____
_____
_____
_____
_____
_____

Devina H. Collier

Rise and Shine

Day 36: The Calling of the Elect

The Lord is not slack concerning his promise, as some men count slackness; but is long suffering toward us, not willing that any should perish, but that all should come to repentance.
2 Peter 3:9

What does it mean to be the "elect" of God? Is it like our process of electing a president or public official? Not at all. For starters, God's "election" includes every man and woman ever created—those who have been called according to His purpose.

As we accept the Lord's call to receive Jesus as our Savior, we become a part of His chosen people. We are set apart for His glory. And that calling comes with a set of expectations that includes kindness, humility, meekness, and long suffering.

The Lord bears with us every single minute. Our shortcomings do not cause Him to waver in His love for us. Yet, how often do we waver in our love

Devina H. Collier

for others, especially when they've sinned against us – including family members?

When we have a complaint against anyone, the Bible urges us to forgive as Christ has forgiven. Ephesians 4:31-32 says: *Let all bitterness, and wrath, and anger, and clamour, and evil speaking, be put away from you, with all malice: And be ye kind one to another, tenderhearted, forgiving one another, even as God for Christ's sake hath forgiven you.*

Which of the virtues listed in Colossians 3:12-13 is more difficult for you to "put on"? Is it humility? Mercy? Choose one virtue to be your focus word this week. Look up Scriptures that apply to it and pray for God to do a mighty work in you.

Prayer and Action Steps:

_____
_____
_____
_____
_____
_____
_____
_____
_____

Devina H. Collier

Anger
Day 37: Warning from God

Be not hasty in thy spirit to be angry: for anger resteth in the bosom of fools.
Ecclesiastes 7:9

A quick temper often stems from a person's striving to maintain control. Anger becomes a coping mechanism when something threatens their sense of authority. A person bound by sinful anger is "eager" to display their wrath. However, for the person on the receiving end of that wrath, it is an awful experience. Walls go up, trust is broken, and eventually, the relationship is put in jeopardy.

My sisters, persistent, sinful anger is straight from the enemy! Genesis 4 describes just how destructive it can be.

So the Lord said to Cain, "Why are you angry? And why has your countenance fallen? If you do well, will you not be accepted? And if you do not do well, sin lies at the door. And its desire is for you, but you should rule over it." Now Cain talked with

Devina H. Collier

Abel his brother; and it came to pass, when they were in the field, that Cain rose up against Abel his brother and killed him. (Genesis 4:6-8)

What I find so tragic about this account, isn't just Abel's senseless death, but Cain's resistance to God's divine warning. Cain had been given the perfect solution from the Lord—a word of deliverance—but he chose to ignore it. He simply rejected knowledge and wisdom.

Sisters, how often are we given clear guidance from the Holy Spirit, to overcome our strongholds, only to ignore Him and move forward with our intentions?

What is your biggest struggle with sin? Is it anger? Pride? Gluttony? Whatever your stronghold is, write it down in RED ink. Each time you struggle with that particular sin, go to your prayer closet and ask God to guide you. Listen carefully for His direction and choose to follow it. Let the red ink remind you that our sins are like scarlet, but Jesus washes us white as snow. (Isaiah 1:18)

Prayer and Action Steps:

_____

_____

_____

Rise and Shine

Devina H. Collier

Day 38: Willing to Yield

Where do wars and fights come from among you? Do they not come from your desires for pleasure that war in your members? You lust and do not have. You murder and covet and cannot obtain. You fight and war. Yet you do not have because you do not ask.
James 4:1-2

James, the brother of Jesus, appealed to his fellow brethren. And he didn't mince words when he pointed out the underlying reasons for contentions and discord. *Lust, murder, and covetousness* were the words he used in defining their motivations.

Ladies, what makes us combative and argumentative? Is it because we don't get what we want? When things don't go our way, do we fight to make it happen?

My sisters, this should not be! There is a beautiful verse in James 3:17 that says, *"But the wisdom that is from above is first pure, then peaceable, gentle, willing to yield, full of mercy and good fruits, without partiality and without hypocrisy."*

 Devina H. Collier

When we are willing to yield to one another in brotherly love, we become instruments of peace. Petty arguments go by the wayside. Selfish ambitions dissipate. Let's ask God for *His* wisdom to become women who are peaceable instead of provoking.

During your devotions, write up to 12 ways you can yield to brotherly love from Leviticus 19:18. Proverbs 17:9. Proverbs 24:17-18, and Matt. 25:35-39.

Prayer and Action Steps:

What?	How?
1.	
2.	
3.	
4.	
5.	
6.	
7.	
8.	
9.	
10.	
11.	
12.	

Devina H. Collier

Day 39: Righteous and Unrighteous Anger

So then, my beloved brethren, let every man be swift to hear, slow to speak, slow to wrath; for the wrath of man does not produce the righteousness of God.
James 1:19-20

There is a righteous anger, that was displayed when Jesus overturned the tables of the moneychangers in the temple. (Matthew 21:12) His zeal for His Father's house spurred Him to portray justice in the form of righteous indignation.

But there is a wrath that does not produce the righteousness of God. It is deep-seeded anger that is reckless. This type of anger is without purpose. It's only goal is to exert one's self-will. If you've ever experienced someone's out-of-control-anger, you know *exactly* what I'm talking about. Explosive anger has no place in our lives. It is destructive to our health and well-being.

There is some truth to the old phrase, "count to ten." It gives time for the nerves, and the mind to

Devina H. Collier

process the emotion and allows time for the adrenals and liver to bring down the spike in stress.

Taking deep breathes and quoting a bible scripture is a more excellent way in dealing with immediate anger.

Choose a Scripture passage to say aloud when irrational anger strikes. Let God's Word be your "count to ten" way of dealing with uncontrolled wrath. Before long, your quick temper will be replaced with the serenity of God's truth and you will no longer be bound by destructive anger.

Prayer and Action Steps:

_____

_____

_____

_____

_____

_____

_____

_____

_____

_____

_____

_____

_____

_____

_____

_____

_____
_____
_____
_____
_____
_____
_____
_____
_____
_____
_____
_____
_____
_____
_____
_____
_____
_____
_____
_____
_____
_____
_____
_____
_____
_____
_____

Day 40: Prudence

I, wisdom, dwell with prudence,
And find out knowledge and discretion.
Proverbs 8:12

Have you ever been seething inside, but had to keep your cool in front of others? Perhaps, it was while dealing with customer service. Or, maybe it was at work, while trying to bear with a difficult person.

Whatever the circumstance, it's what we do with those intense emotions that matter. We have a choice. Are we going to allow frustration to get the best of us? Or, are we going to let the fruit of the Holy Spirit shine through?

Prudence means having discernment. Being able to calmly and tactfully handle feelings of frustration wisely. It is a sign of self-control and maturity.

How difficult is it for you to hold your tongue? Are you quick to exhibit irritation? Begin to pray for a prudent heart—a heart that is willing to respond instead of reacting.

Devina H. Collier

In the first column, write your typical response to frustrating situations (yelling, throwing things, etc.) In the second column, write alternative actions you can take (going outside for fresh air, getting a drink of water, etc.) On purpose, utilize prudence.

Frustration Response	Alternative Action

Day 41: The Enemy's Foothold

  Devina H. Collier

*Be angry, and do not sin. Do not let the sun go
down on your wrath, nor give place to the devil.
Ephesians 4:26-27*

There is a strong tendency to justify our anger and
stubbornly refuse to let things go. We think that if
we hold on to a grudge long enough, it will
somehow change the situation.

But what really happens, as the sun goes down on
our anger, is that the enemy gets a foothold and
harass us. Remember, Satan wants nothing more
than to steal, kill, and destroy. Have you ever
noticed that your issues tend to get blown out of
proportion in the night? Simple, solvable problems
seem monumental during the night watches.
That's because we have given the enemy
opportunity to mess with us when all we need to
do is quote God's word or repeat out loud the
name of Jesus.

*"Be angry, and do not sin" do not let the sun go
down on your wrath, 27 nor give place to the
devil." (Ephesians 4:26)*
Sisters, for our ultimate health and well-being, we
must learn to deal with our emotions promptly and

directly. We must resolve them in our minds before they blossom into something bigger.

We will get angry. And not everything in life will be resolved instantly. However, we have the choice to deal with our emotional responses *before* the devil gets a foothold.

This week, try to deal with negative emotions before bed. Fill your mind with words of truth. Try listening to a Bible App as you fall asleep or play 24 hours gospel music in your bedroom. The Proverbs or Psalms are a good way to soothe emotional distress and restrain the devil from getting a foothold.

Prayer and Action Steps:

_____
_____
_____
_____
_____
_____
_____
_____
_____
_____
_____

_____
_____
_____
_____
_____
_____
_____
_____
_____
_____
_____
_____
_____
_____
_____
_____
_____
_____
_____
_____
_____
_____
_____
_____
_____

Fear Not

Day 42: Abiding in Perfect Love

*There is no fear in love; but perfect love casteth
out fear: because fear hath torment.
He that feareth is not made perfect in love.
1 John 4:18*

There is a beautiful passage of Scripture that precedes our key verse for today. It speaks of abiding in the Savior and knowing He abides in us.

By this we know that we abide in Him, and He in us, because He has given us of His Spirit. And we have seen and testify that the Father has sent the Son as Savior of the world. Whoever confesses that Jesus is the Son of God, God abides in him, and he in God. (1 John 4:13-15)

My sisters, because we have the Holy Spirit, we are assured of Christ's perfect love in us. When we are dominated by a spirit of fear, doubt, or torment, it is at those times when we need to ask ourselves. Am I abiding in Jesus, or am I following Him only sometimes?

Devina H. Collier

The enemy has legal ground to harass us if we say and do things contrary to the Holy Spirit. For example, if we slander someone, and don't repent or turn from it, that can allow the enemy to swiftly torment us day and night. Thank God, ladies that we have the Holy Spirit to convict us, so we know when to repent.

Remember, perfect love casts out fear. And what is perfect love? Jesus Christ Himself!

Do you have Jesus? If you are able to answer, "yes," then you are FREE from the oppressive bonds of fear. Allow the matchless love of Christ to be perfected in you.

Go on a nature walk and find a small branch. Bring it home and place it on a shelf where you will see it often. Let that branch be a reminder to abide in the True Vine. His love is made perfect in you! Write the dears that trouble you. Then cross it out and write over it "I am abiding in the True Vine!" Amen.

Prayer and Action Steps:

_____
_____
_____
_____

Rise and Shine

Day 43: Solid Rock

*I will say unto God my rock, why hast thou
forgotten me? Why go I mourning because
of the oppression of the enemy?*
Psalm 42:9

Have you ever been forgotten? Perhaps, your birthday came and went without acknowledgement from a loved one. Or, maybe you had plans to meet a friend, but they never showed. It's not a pleasant feeling to be forgotten.

If we're completely honest, it sometimes feels as if we've been forgotten by God. We may even feel like the enemy has gained the upper hand. When our best intentions fall apart, and things don't work out, we may assume that God has forgotten us.

Take heart, sisters! No matter how we feel, God is our Rock! He is our sure foundation—our refuge in times of trouble. And the enemy cannot oppress us when we are standing on the Rock of our salvation.

Devina H. Collier

Do you believe this today? Are you standing firm on Jesus Christ? Then do not believe the lie that God has forgotten you. When those feelings come, stand firm and declare,

"On Christ the Solid Rock I stand! All other ground is sinking sand!"

Listen to the old hymn, "On Christ the Solid Rock I Stand," and let that be your victory song today. Write a prayer thanking God for helping you to stand. Then list 10 events in your life that God has not forgotten you.

Prayer and Action Steps:

_____
_____
_____
_____
_____
_____
_____
_____
_____
_____
_____
_____
_____

    Devina H. Collier

Devina H. Collier

Day 44: His Mighty Power

And when he had called unto him his twelve disciples, he gave them power against unclean spirits, to cast them out, and to heal all manner of sickness and all manner of disease.
Matthew 10:1

What a powerful, powerful verse this is for us, ladies! The mighty gifts of healing that Jesus bestowed on His disciples were capable of eliminating all manner of sickness and disease. And just in case you've forgotten, we, also, are disciples of the Most High God!

The Lord has given each of us His Spirit, full of wisdom, knowledge, and power. In our health and life, we have every resource needed to cast out what doesn't belong and fill ourselves with the best God has to offer.

Are you sick today? Call the elders of your church to pray over you and anoint you with oil. (James 5:14-15) Enlist a prayer team of trusted friends who will cover you with petitions of faith.

Most of all, my friends, believe that Jesus is mighty to save! He can heal, defend, and restore every oppressive thing in your life. Will you declare that today? Let's live as Christ's disciples, full of the Holy Spirit's power to cast out every unclean spirit—all in the beautiful Name of Jesus!

From the word D-I-S-C-I-P-L-E. Think of a powerful word for each letter and write it in bold letters. Perhaps "D" can stand for DECISION, or the letter "I" for INVINCIBLE. Let these declarations remind you that you are a disciple of Jesus Christ!

Prayer and Action Steps:

D	
I	
S	
C	
I	
P	
L	
E	

Day 45: Christ, Our Righteousness

*The Lord executes righteousness and
Justice for all who are oppressed.
Psalm 103:6*

There is nothing more satisfying than seeing justice upheld. In a world where injustice plays such a big role, it's wonderful to see equity thrive.

Our good and gracious Father does all of that for us. He has the authority to grant mercy over every unjust thing we are facing. We are not sentenced to a life of oppression. The Lord has already executed righteousness on our behalf, and His verdict was Jesus' death on the cross.

What shall we then say to these things? If God be for us, who can be against us? He that spared not his own Son, but delivered him up for us all, how shall he not with him also freely give us all things? (Romans 8:31-32)

Ladies, there is nothing that can keep us down! We have the most powerful Advocate, standing on our behalf. We don't have to worry about

 Devina H. Collier

injustice. The ruling, in our favor, has already been given!

Jesus is our righteousness, our sanctification, and our redemption. And that is something we can boldly proclaim in the face of oppression.

What injustice in this world bothers you most? Is it helping the sick? Battered women? Orphans? Pray about getting involved with a local or national ministry. Fight for those who desperately need justice to prevail.

Prayer and Action Steps:

_____

_____

_____

_____

_____

_____

_____

_____

_____

_____

_____

_____

_____

_____

_____

_____

Habits

Day 46: Out of the Heart

And he said, that which cometh out of the man, that defileth the man. For from within, out of the heart of men, proceed evil thoughts, adulteries, fornications, murders, thefts, covetousness, wickedness, deceit, lasciviousness, an evil eye, blasphemy, pride, foolishness: all these evil things come from within, and defile the man.
Mark 7:20-23

All of us struggle with making good food choices. Sometimes it's a test to say "no" to a bag of chips or an extra slice of cake. However, the essence of our poor choices comes from an unresolved issue *within*, not from without.

Think about it. How often do our negative thoughts or stress related situations lead us to reach for those comfort foods? Ladies, you should know that fleshly desire can lead us astray. It's not only our flesh that leads us astray, but our hearts as well. Once we grasp the importance of being transformed in the deepest part of ourselves, we can then begin to make choices based on truth.

Defilement, in the Old Testament, had to do with physical things that made the body unclean. When Jesus came, He made it clear to the Pharisees that it was not the outside elements they were to be concerned about. Instead, He warned them of the evil that comes from within.

And he saith unto them, Are ye so without understanding also? Do ye not perceive, that whatsoever thing from without entereth into the man, it cannot defile him; because it entereth not into his heart, but into the belly, and goeth out into the draught, purging all meats? Mark 7:18-19

Sisters, it is highly important that we recognize what is going on *inside* us that leads to poor habits. When we ignore our inner motives, we will continue to make unhealthy choices.

Every time you are tempted to reach for "comfort foods," write down your thoughts, emotions, and stress levels at that exact moment. You might begin to see a pattern! Write some good habits you can think of that can replace the bad habits.

Prayer and Action Steps:

_____

_____

_____

Rise and Shine

Day 47: Vibrant for His Purpose

And be not conformed to this world: but be ye transformed by the renewing of your mind, That ye may prove what is that good, and acceptable, and perfect, will of God.
Romans 12:2

Have you ever wondered if God really cares about our personal habits? Especially in the area of eating, drinking, and exercise, is the Lord concerned with how we treat our bodies?

You bet He does!

The Bible tells us again and again that God's ultimate purpose for mankind is for them to believe in the name of His Son and receive Him that they might have eternal life. (See John 3:16-18, Acts 16:31, 1 Peter 1:8-9)

So, how does this relate to taking good care of our bodies?

My sisters, if we are instruments of God's love, called to share the Good News of the Gospel with others, how can we do that effectively when we are sick and tired?

If we don't drink water and are filling our bodies with processed foods that have no nutritional value, we aren't going to have the energy needed to be the best we can be for Christ. Instead, we are going to feel tired and sluggish, desiring more of the foods that made us feel sick in the first place. This might be a good time to get out the trash can and start eliminating processed foods from your kitchen pantry.

When we forsake the temptations of this world, and allow the Holy Spirit to renew our minds, we can then see clearly God's good, pleasing, and perfect will and walk in it. No longer will we be caught up in the vicious cycle of our habits.

God does care about our personal habits. He longs for us to be our best selves because then we can be vibrant and healthy for His divine purpose. Are you ready to step out of destructive habits and into His will?

Today's action plan is a big one. Please don't skip this step! Take one hour to clean out your cabinets, refrigerator, and pantry. Box up or throw away EVERYTHING that is not good for you.

Don't think about it—just do it. Then, make a list of healthy things you will buy to replace those foods. This is the start of a brand, new you!

Prayer and Action Steps:

_____

_____

_____

_____

_____

_____

_____

_____

_____

_____

_____

_____

_____

_____

_____

_____

_____

_____

_____

_____

_____

_____

Day 48: You Have Overcome!

Ye are of God, little children, and have overcome them: because greater is He that is in you, than he that is in the world.
1 John 4:4

When the challenges of life keep us busy, our commitment can sometimes evade us, but greater is He that is in you, than he that is in the world. That verse is the KEY to our victory over temptation! Do you believe that today? Even when we feel weak, God is not. When we feel defeated, Christ is victorious. And by the power of the Holy Spirit in us, we have the strength to make the best choices.

Ladies, we have overcome! We are overcomers by the blood of the Lamb and the word of His testimony.

And I heard a loud voice saying in heaven, Now is come salvation, and strength, and the kingdom of our God, and the power of his Christ: for the accuser of our brethren is cast down, which accused them before our God day and night.

And they overcame him by the blood of the Lamb, and by the word of their testimony; and they loved not their lives unto the death. Revelation 12:10-11

Christ's power has defeated the one who tempts us. We just need to take hold of that victory and never let go!

Write down the following statements from the Bible. End each statement with an exclamation point, declaring that you are an overcomer!

- Greater is He that is in me, than he who is in the world!
- Our accuser is cast down forever!
- We have overcome by the blood of the Lamb!

Prayer and Action Steps:

_____

_____

_____

_____

_____

_____

_____

_____

_____

Rise and Shine

Devina H. Collier

Day 49: Follow the Signs

There hath no temptation taken you but such as is common to man: but God is faithful, who will not suffer you to be tempted above that ye are able; but will with the temptation also make a way to escape, that ye may be able to bear it.
1 Corinthians 10:13

What would happen if we ignored road signs? If we drove straight through stop signs, cruised through yields, or drove the opposite way down a one-way street, what would eventually happen?

We would crash!

So, it is with our habits, my friends. We are tempted, daily, to ignore the road signs of health. In fact, God gives us a sign that says, "This Way" each time we face temptation. We just need to be better at following His road sign.

Although strongholds can feel mightily powerful, they aren't stronger than we can bear. We can count on God to provide an alternative route. By first stopping to ask for the Lord's direction, we will avoid the temptations common to man.

The very next time your focus is off, STOP what you are doing. YIELD to the Holy Spirit. And make a U-TURN in the direction God wants you to go. List some action steps you can take that can help you stay focused.

Prayer and Action Steps:

_____
_____
_____
_____
_____
_____
_____
_____
_____
_____
_____
_____
_____
_____
_____
_____
_____
_____
_____
_____

Devina H. Collier

Day 50: Feast on the Word

My son, attend to my words; incline thine ear unto my sayings. Let them not depart from thine eyes; keep them in the midst of thine heart. For they are life unto those that find them, and health to all their flesh.
Proverbs 4:20-22

Did you know that the Word of God is foundational to our health and well-being? Every word from the mouth of the Lord is useful and life-giving. Far more than ink on the page, the Scriptures are living and active, able to penetrate soul and spirit, joints and marrow.

For the word of God is quick, and powerful, and sharper than any twoedged sword, piercing even to the dividing asunder of soul and spirit, and of the joints and marrow, and is a discerner of the thoughts and intents of the heart. (Hebrews 4:12)

Often, we mistake the Bible as only beneficial to our spiritual health. But sisters, it is the ultimate guidebook for every part of our being. We cannot separate our hearts from our bodies or our souls from our minds. ALL those things make us who we are. The Word of God can penetrate the deepest parts.

Ladies, let us feast on the life-giving wisdom of God! Let us crave His Word more than our daily bread. Let us devote as much time as possible reading and meditating upon the Lord's life-giving statutes.

Incline your ears unto the sayings of the Lord, knowing they are vital to your spiritual and physical health. Give God praise! Tell Him how much you love Him. Write down and memorize 3 John 2. "Beloved, I pray that you may prosper in all things and be in health, just as your soul prospers."

Prayer and Action Steps:

_____
_____
_____
_____
_____
_____
_____
_____
_____
_____
_____

Honor to His Name
Day 51: Edification

*Let the words of my mouth, and the meditation
of my heart, be acceptable in thy sight,
O Lord, my strength, and my redeemer.*
Psalm 19:14

Perhaps you've heard of the children's Bible school lesson, where the teacher squeezes out toothpaste and then asks the students to try to put it back in the tube. The heart of the lesson is that you can't take back your words once you speak them.

When David petitioned of the Lord, he asked for acceptable words and meditations of the heart. So, what words are considered acceptable to God? What thoughts bring honor to His name?

Let no corrupt communication proceed out of your mouth, but that which is good to the use of edifying, that it may minister grace unto the hearers. Ephesians 4:29

Devina H. Collier

Words that build others up and minister grace are acceptable words. Foul language, foolish arguments, and sharp sarcasm are the things that tear down.

Set your affection on things above, not on things on the earth. Colossians 3:2

Thoughts that focus on heavenly things and not the things of this world are acceptable thoughts. Entertaining unhealthy ideas, not only can make the mind (soul) sick, but also organs too.

Unfortunately, we are bombarded with words and images that do not glorify God. Just driving down the street, we see and hear things that are not acceptable to the Lord. That is why, like King David, we must petition the Lord and ask Him to guard the meditations of our hearts. For our hearts are the wellspring of life. *Keep thy heart with all diligence; for out of it are the issues of life. (Proverbs 4:23)*

May the words of our mouths and the meditations of our hearts be acceptable to God, our strength and our Redeemer.

Pay close attention to the words you use. Filter out anything that does not glorify God or edify others. Be intentional about building others up instead of criticizing them. Fill your mind with useful things such as worship music, Christian podcasts, and Scriptures.

Ask God in prayer to strip the desire of negative words off your soul, body and spirit. Consider removing from your home movies, music, CDs, magazines, and gifts that give the enemy legal ground to tempt you into dwelling on or using negative words. Replace those things with more excellent things that give no place to the enemy. List the items you would like to have.

Prayer and Action Steps:

_____
_____
_____
_____
_____
_____
_____
_____
_____
_____
_____
_____
_____
_____
_____
_____

Rise and Shine

Day 52: Two-By-Four Vision

And why do you look at the speck in your brother's eye, but do not consider the plank in your own eye? Or how can you say to your brother, 'Let me remove the speck from your eye'; and look, a plank is in your own eye?
Matthew 7:3-4

As you probably know, a person who is nearsighted can see things better close up, while a person who is farsighted can clearly see things far away.

Unfortunately, I'm afraid many of us are terribly farsighted. We can easily spot another person's sin from across the room, but our vision becomes blurred when we look in the mirror.

When Jesus spoke from the mountaintop, he warned the multitudes against judging others. He wasn't saying that we can never point out a destructive behavior, but He was saying that we must first, remove the two-by-four from our own eye so that we can clearly see the twig in our brother's eye.

What a wealth of wisdom this is for us, ladies! By first acknowledging our own sin, and doing whatever it takes to remove it, we are then free to lovingly confront someone else.

No one likes to feel judged. Relationships crumble when one person constantly feels criticized. And our words are completely ineffective if we have not dealt with the sin in our own lives. In essence, we become hypocrites.

Ask the Lord for "Spiritual glasses" to see things close up. Ask Him to remove any farsightedness in your life.

How have you been judgmental toward someone? Schedule a time to meet with that person and apologize. Let them know that you struggle with issues as well, and that together you can work toward removing strongholds. If you feel uneasy about meeting face-to-face, write a letter instead.

Prayer and Action Steps:

_____
_____
_____
_____
_____
_____

Rise and Shine

Devina H. Collier

Day 53: Hurts

*He that goeth about as a talebearer
revealeth secrets: therefore meddle not
with him that flattereth with his lips.*
Proverbs 20:19

If you've ever been on the receiving end of gossip, you've probably sensed the forewarning of the Holy Spirit to end the conversation immediately. Even though we are all tempted to mutter things we shouldn't, we know that gossip damages relationships.

Trust is an essential piece in building strong and healthy friendships. We need to know that things we've shared in confidence won't be revealed to others. And, our loved ones need to be assured that we won't go around spreading things they've shared with us.

Avoid gossip at all cost. It doesn't glorify God or edify the body. Before you jump into an unhealthy conversation, heed the Holy Spirit's warning and bite your tongue. Change the subject, leave the room, or do whatever you need to prevent gossip from continuing.

Is gossip a struggle for you? Take some time to think about why you feel the need to talk about others. Is it to make yourself look better? Is it because it somehow makes you feel superior? These are tough questions to answer, but I encourage you to face this issue head-on and make real strides in eradicating gossip from your life. Write the steps you can take to avoid gossip when you hear someone else gossiping.

Prayer and Action Steps:

_____
_____
_____
_____
_____
_____
_____
_____
_____
_____
_____
_____
_____
_____

Devina H. Collier

Day 54: Ill-planned Advice

He that answereth a matter before he heareth it, it is folly and shame unto him.
Proverbs 18:13

Do you like to give advice? Are you good at counseling others? A solid mentor will listen intently before offering guidance. Even the most well-meaning advice can be more hurtful than good when given too hastily. In fact, some people come across as "know-it-alls" when they are set on stating their opinion.

Relationships thrive when *both* parties feel heard and valued. Let's be quick to listen and careful to speak. Here are a few questions to ask yourself before you launch into "counselor mode."

- Is my advice Biblical?
- Does my advice relate specifically to their situation?
- Is it offered in a spirit of love?

There is nothing wrong with being a mentor to someone. In fact, God calls many of us to mentor others in wisdom and truth. However, He also calls us to listen carefully. If we are just trying to get our opinion out there, it would be better for us to keep our words to ourselves.

As you meet with friends, make it a goal to listen well. Don't be too hasty to answer. Instead, try asking them thought-provoking questions that will turn the conversation toward biblical truths and lead them in God-honoring wisdom. In prayer ask the Lord to be your ears and mouth and to speak what He want you to say. Write down action steps you can take, such as letting them know that you will get back to them after you have had time to think through it.

Prayer and Action Steps:

_____
_____
_____
_____
_____
_____
_____
_____
_____
_____
_____
_____

Day 55: As far as it Depends on You

Recompense to no man evil for evil.
Provide things honest in the sight of all men.
If it be possible, as much as lieth in you,
live peaceably with all men.
Romans 12:17-18

So much of what it takes to have healthy relationships depends on us. The Bible encourages," *as far as it depends on you, live in peace with all men.*"

It takes intentionality to live peaceably. Especially when we've been wronged, it's part of our human nature to retaliate. However, as "Jesus followers," we no longer live according to our human nature. We live according to the Holy Spirit.

For they that are after the flesh do mind the things of the flesh; but they that are after the Spirit the things of the Spirit. (Romans 8:5)

There will be the rare occasion when living peaceably won't be possible—not because we aren't doing everything we can do, but because the other person is unwilling. Those situations call for great discernment and prayer and may eventually lead to parting ways. However, honesty, integrity, and a spirit of forgiveness will go a long way in maintaining healthy relationships. As far as it depends on you, live at peace.

Is there a current conflict with someone in your life? How are you handling it? Determine to promote peace and avoid foolish arguments that lead to dissension. As time goes on, the other person will notice your efforts to maintain harmony in the relationship. And hopefully, they will respond likewise. Pray for peace and write the steps you will take to keep your peace when problems arise.

Prayer and Action Steps:

_____
_____
_____
_____
_____
_____
_____
_____
_____
_____
_____

Devina H. Collier

_____
_____
_____
_____
_____
_____
_____
_____
_____
_____
_____
_____
_____
_____
_____
_____
_____
_____
_____
_____
_____
_____
_____
_____
_____

Priorities

Day 56: Thorough Examination

Examine me, O Lord, and prove me; try my mind and my heart. For Your lovingkindness is before my eyes, and I have walked in Your truth.
Psalm 26:2-3

Examinations are rarely pleasant. No one enjoys going to the doctor for a check-up. It requires stepping on that dreaded scale, answering questions about our habits, getting blood work done, and waiting for results.

So, when David asked the Lord to examine him, to prove that his mind and heart were full of integrity, he was making himself vulnerable to the Lord's evaluation. Because He desired to live according to God's truths, David was willing to let an in-depth examination take place.

An intimate relationship with the Lord allows for regular examinations. When we are completely devoted to Him, we are willing to let Him shine His light of truth into every facet of our being.

Keep in mind, sisters, that the Lord examines us with loving kindness, leading us to the repentance of anything that is contrary to His Word.

Has it been a while since you knew what your own health needs were? Do you take care of everyone else's health needs first, instead of your own? Do you seek answers from man more than answers from God about your health?

Do you actively ask God to lead you into wellness? Are you willing to be patient, and work out the steps God has for your healing? Are you willing to face whatever lifestyle changes He prompts you to take? It may be just what you need to get on track and set your priorities straight.

Let it be the petition of our hearts to allow the Lord to "try us" and prove our faithfulness to Him. Pray and write down what you sense God is leading you to do about your health.

Prayer and Action Steps:

_____
_____
_____
_____
_____
_____

Rise and Shine

Devina H. Collier

Day 57: Accountable for Every Action

Wherefore we labour, that, whether present or absent, we may be accepted of him. For we must all appear before the judgment seat of Christ; that every one may receive the things done in his body, according to that he hath done, whether it be good or bad.
2 Corinthians 5:9-10

There are many things we do on a regular basis without even thinking. We forget that our day-to-day activities matter to God. The Bible tells us that we will be accountable for every action we take and for every word we speak.

But I say to you that for every idle word men may speak, they will give account of it in the day of judgment. Matthew 12:36

Sisters, this is not to be confused with trying to live a perfect life or earn our salvation. Remember, we do good works, not to get saved, but because we are saved. As Christian women, it should be our goal to please the Lord because we love Him.

Devina H. Collier

In these rows of Heart, Mind, Soul, and Strength. Write down your current thoughts, words, and actions. Things like resentment, dishonesty, or hidden sins may come to light as you do this exercise. Be honest with yourself and with God. Commit to live intentionally, bringing everything under His authority.

Prayer and Action Steps:

Heart Mind (Soul)	
Strength	

Day 58: Make Time for God

"...that ye might be filled with the knowledge of his will in all wisdom and spiritual understanding; that ye might walk worthy of the Lord unto all pleasing, being fruitful in every good work, and increasing in the knowledge of God;
Colossians 1:9-10

In the hectic pace of life, many of us feel like we are barely keeping our heads above water. It seems like we are on the run from morning to night. Some days schedules leave little room for Bible study and communion with the Lord.

My sisters, no matter what you need to eliminate from your schedule, daily time with God is a must! There is no room for compromise. If we want our lives to be fruitful, we absolutely must make God's Word, prayer, and worship a priority.

Having a successful job or living the all-American dream, pales in comparison to being filled with spiritual understanding. Everything on earth is as *nothing* compared to walking worthy of the Lord.

How have you let the "busyness" of life overtake you? Spending time with God is going to anchor you through the busyness of life.

Be encouraged today. It's never too late to reprioritize your life. Bit by bit, you can make the necessary changes to put God first and begin living a life that is pleasing to Him.

Take a good look at your calendar for the next 3 months. At a glance, what things do you see that can be rearranged or eliminated altogether? Form a 90-day plan that will get you and your family on track. Schedule quiet times with the Lord and treat those times as very important appointments.

Prayer and Action Steps:

_____
_____
_____
_____
_____
_____
_____
_____
_____
_____
_____

Day 59: All Your Might

*And thou shalt love the Lord thy God with
all thine heart, and with all thy soul,
and with all thy might.
Deuteronomy 6:5*

What has been the most challenging physical things you've ever done in your life? Perhaps, it was running a half-marathon. Or, maybe you lost a tremendous amount of weight. It might have been that you overcame an addiction or sickness. Whatever your greatest physical challenge, what did it take for you to achieve it? I would guess that your answer would be "determination."

So, here's a tough question: Have you loved God with the same kind of determination? Stop at nothing. The inheritance of heaven is worth it.

Part of what motivates us to work hard for something, is an intense desire for a particular outcome. We desire to lose weight, so we make healthy food choices and get plenty of exercise. We desire to make more money, so we work extra hours. But how much do we desire God?

Devina H. Collier

Sisters, an intense desire to grow closer to the Lord is foundational for our Christian walk. And we cultivate that desire by spending time with Him in the Word, worship, and prayer. As we do these things more and more, our desire for Him will grow.

Today, journal about your greatest achievement in life. Write out the things you did to reach your goal. What actions did you take? Where was your focus? What things did you implement into your life to make it happen? Now, on the flip side of that page, write today's verse at the top. What actions will you take to love God with all your might? What things will you implement to make this verse a reality?

Prayer and Action Steps:

_____

_____

_____

_____

_____

_____

_____

_____

_____

_____

_____

 Devina H. Collier

Rise and Shine

Devina H. Collier

Day 60: A Better Way

*Flee also youthful lusts: but follow righteousness,
faith, charity, peace, with them that call
on the Lord out of a pure heart.
2 Timothy 2:22*

Looking back at photos from the past, some of us may laugh at the clothes we wore or the hairstyles we thought were so popular. Our perspectives change as we get older and we leave our youthful ways behind.

However, some of our youthful practices follow us into adulthood. Addictions, habits, beliefs, and prejudices can stick with us well into our adult years. But ladies, youthful lusts have no place in our "born-again" lives. They are not becoming of women who are devoted to God Most High.

In the righteousness of Christ, we are called to walk in faith, charity, and peace. Why, then, do we still carry some of the sinful lusts of the past?

Sisters, it is time to shake off the old and put on the new!

...if indeed you have heard Him and have been taught by Him, as the truth is in Jesus: that you put off, concerning your former conduct, the old man which grows corrupt according to the deceitful lusts, and be renewed in the spirit of your mind, and that you put on the new man which was created according to God, in true righteousness and holiness. (Ephesians 4:21-14)

Jesus has taught us to put off our former conduct, our deceitful lusts, and the things that corrupt. We are to put on the new, created by God in righteousness and holiness. This indicates an action on our part. We must be proactive in discerning what youthful sins still remain and take the proper actions to remove them.

Look through an old photo album and thank God for bringing you out of darkness and into His glorious light. Commit to leaving the former ways of youth behind. Ask the Lord to help you let go of past sins and put on His righteousness and holiness. Tell Him to strip it off your body, mind (soul), and spirit. Write the steps you can take to walk in boldness.

Prayer and Action Steps:

_____

_____

_____
_____
_____
_____
_____
_____
_____
_____
_____
_____
_____
_____
_____
_____
_____
_____
_____
_____
_____
_____
_____
_____
_____
_____
_____

Grief

Day 61: The Pain of Heartbreak

The Lord is near to those who have a broken heart, And saves such as have a contrite spirit.
Psalm 34:18

Heartbreak is, perhaps, one of the most painful feelings a human being can endure. Within the deepest part of ourselves, anguish radiates through every fiber of our being and we are rocked to the core. Ladies, it's important not to vent it wrongly or suppress it because our health can be affected by it.

It may be our tendency to mask our true feelings and attempt to stoically move forward in our own strength. However, the Bible encourages us to humbly go before the Lord and bring every hurt to Him. He invites us to come before His throne and pour out our hearts, freely crying out in our pain and distress.

In my distress I called upon the Lord, and cried out to my God; He heard my voice from His temple, and my cry came before Him, even to His ears.
Psalm 18:6

 Devina H. Collier

One of the most beautiful word pictures in the Bible, Revelation 8:4, describes our prayers like incense before God's throne. As our brokenhearted prayers ascend, like a beautiful fragrance, the Lord hears and draws near.

My sisters, the Lord sees your contrite spirit. He is close to your broken heart. Will you be humble before Him? Will you cast all your cares upon Him, knowing He cares for you?

Go to your prayer closet and hold nothing back. Let the pain of your heartbreak flow into the hands of the Living God. Call on Him to save you from your distress. The Lord your God is with you!

Prayer:

_____
_____
_____
_____
_____
_____
_____
_____
_____
_____
_____
_____
_____
_____
_____
_____
_____
_____
_____
_____
_____
_____
_____
_____
_____
_____
_____
_____

Day 62: The Helper

I, even I, am he that comforteth you: who art
thou, that thou shouldest be afraid of a man
that shall die, and of the son of man
which shall be made as grass;
Isaiah 51:12

What I like about storms is that they do pass. If you
are dealing with a storm right now because of a
loved one, a job loss, health challenge or medical
bills. Whatever the reason, the comfort of Jesus will
bless you and everything will work out for your
good. The word blessed, in Greek, is *Makarios,*
which means that God *extends* His benefits and
lengthens His mercies towards us.

Before Jesus' death, He promised his disciples a
Comforter—One who would be with them to
encourage and guide.

*And I will pray the Father, and He will give you
another Helper, that He may abide with you
forever—the Spirit of truth, whom the world cannot
receive, because it neither sees Him, nor knows
Him; but you know Him, for He dwells with you and
will be with you. I will not leave you orphans; I will
come to you. (John 14:16-18)*

Devina H. Collier

What a comforting truth! The Spirit of God is with us through every season of grief. In the dark places, the lonely places, and the hurting places, He is there.

Dear one, are you experiencing intense storms? Be encouraged today. Know that the Spirit of the Lord is with you. He is your Helper and your Comforter. Read Romans 8:26 and write down the promise of the Holy Spirit. Cling to this truth in your storm.

Prayer and Action Steps:

_____
_____
_____
_____
_____
_____
_____
_____
_____
_____
_____
_____
_____

Day 63: God of ALL Comfort

Devina H. Collier

*Blessed be God, even the Father of our Lord
Jesus Christ, the Father of mercies, and the
God of all comfort; who comforteth us in all
our tribulation, that we may be able to comfort
them which are in any trouble, by the comfort
wherewith we ourselves are comforted of God.
2 Corinthians 1:3-4*

Why does God allow difficult things to happen?
Why there are trials and tribulations? Wouldn't it
be wonderful if we were promised carefree lives
of comfort and ease? Sure, it would but then we
wouldn't need God. We are needy. We couldn't
breathe without the help of the Lord.

There are many things we will not understand this
side of heaven. But one thing we know for sure—
God is the Father of mercies. The Bible doesn't say
He is the God of "some" comfort. No, the Bible
declares that He is the God of ALL comfort!

The Lord allows us to go through trials, not only to
build our faith, but to equip us to help others. How
often have we gone through a trial, only to meet
someone who has already been through it? Those
people become sources of comfort for us. They

Devina H. Collier

are able to help us navigate through the tough seasons.

Sisters, try to view your trials in a new light. Ask the Lord for understanding, that you might be able to help someone else who is going through the same thing.

How can you begin to help others in your church or community? Perhaps, your church has a grief counseling ministry. Or, maybe your community has volunteer counseling services. Pray about getting involved. You have something to give back. God may want to use you to comfort others in their trial.

Prayer and Action Steps:

_____

_____

_____

_____

_____

_____

_____

_____

_____

_____

_____

_____

_____
_____
_____
_____
_____
_____
_____
_____
_____
_____
_____
_____
_____
_____
_____
_____
_____
_____
_____
_____
_____
_____
_____
_____
_____

Day 64: Life-giving Word

*Remember the word to Your servant, upon which
You have caused me to hope. This is my comfort
in my affliction, For Your word has given me life.
Psalm 119:49-50*

I heard a story about a man who lost his little girl in
a tragic accident. For many weeks after, he kept
his Bible with him, even sleeping with it on his chest
at night. In his pain, he related that he just needed
to know the Word of God was near. It was his way
of coping with his grief.

That is a beautiful word-picture of the healing
balm that pours out from the Living Word. It's not
the physical book that heals, but the life-giving
words spoken from the mouth of God. My sisters,
the Scriptures are foundational for healing.

It is critical for us to equip our hearts with the
Scriptures; to memorize passages that will comfort
us in times of sorrow. Preparing ahead of time arms
us with words of hope when feelings of
hopelessness come. How has the Bible been of
comfort to you? Do you have certain passages to
turn to in times of grief?

Devina H. Collier

Choose a new passage of Scripture to write out, memorize, and meditate upon. Hide that passage deep in your heart. Say it often, reminding yourself of the life-giving comfort the Word of God brings. Begin to let go of the affliction in prayer. Write 10 related words to hope, such as promise, confidence, the bright side...

Prayer and Action Steps:

_____

_____

_____

_____

_____

_____

_____

_____

_____

_____

_____

_____

_____

_____

_____

_____

_____

_____

_____

_____

_____
_____
_____
_____
_____
_____
_____
_____
_____
_____
_____
_____
_____
_____
_____
_____
_____
_____
_____
_____
_____
_____
_____
_____

Day 65: Momentary Troubles

And God shall wipe away all tears from their eyes; and there shall be no more death, neither sorrow, nor crying, neither shall there be any more pain: for the former things are passed away.
Revelation 21:4

It is difficult to imagine a place where there is no sorrow, pain, or death. As tragic news headlines are broadcast around the world, it's hard to envision all the world's suffering coming to an end.

Revelation 21:4 is a reminder that there will be a day when our current sorrows will pass away. And the very hand of God will remove every tear.

Sisters, our momentary troubles are but for a season. The struggles of this life will see their finality. Just as the apostle Paul stated in 2 Corinthians 4, our momentary afflictions are working out for us a glorious future.

"...but though our outward man perish, yet the inward man is renewed day by day. For our light affliction, which is but for a moment, worketh for us a far more exceeding and eternal weight of glory..."(2 Corinthians 4:16-1)7

Devina H. Collier

Everything around us may feel depressing and overwhelming, however, our "light afflictions" are but for a moment. Eternity with the Savior is forever!

Whatever is troubling your soul today, look ahead to the hope of God's glory. Spend some time reading about heaven, your eternal home, in which there will be no more sorrow, pain, or death.
(See Revelation 5:9-13, 22:1-5). In prayer, give thanks.

Prayer:

_____
_____
_____
_____
_____
_____
_____
_____
_____
_____
_____
_____
_____
_____
_____

Insecurity
Day 66: Every Piece

*Put on the whole armour of God, that ye may
be able to stand against the wiles of the devil.
For we wrestle not against flesh and blood, but
against principalities, against powers, against
the rulers of the darkness of this world, against
spiritual wickedness in high places.
Ephesians 6:11-12*

Soldiers, in the day of battle, would never have forgotten to put on a piece of armor. They wouldn't have left their shields behind, nor their swords, nor their helmets.

My sisters, we are in the day of battle! Not against people, but against the principalities of darkness and the ruler of this dark world. You can bet that Satan doesn't leave any weapon behind. He is out to get us with every bit of ammunition he has.

Lies that entice, doubts that bring fear, and insecurities that paralyze us, are all arrows in the hand of our adversary. He launches them when we are most vulnerable.
But listen, ladies. The enemy of our souls is already DEFEATED! He may think he still has power over us, but Jesus Christ conquered him the moment He

drew His last breath on the cross and three days later rose again.

Sisters, we are only secure in the FULL armor of God. The belt of truth, the breastplate of righteousness, the sword of the Spirit, the shield of faith, the helmet of salvation, and the boots of the Gospel, cover us from head to toe.

Have you put on God's armor today?

What piece of God's armor are you lacking? Read Ephesians 6: 14-17. Make a list of each piece of armor and circle the ones you struggle to put on. Then, take it to the Lord and ask Him to clothe you with everything you need to stand against the arrows of the enemy. List 5 reasons why it is vital to put on the whole armor of God.

Prayer and Action Steps:

_____
_____
_____
_____
_____
_____
_____
_____
_____

Devina H. Collier

_____
_____
_____
_____
_____
_____
_____
_____
_____
_____
_____
_____
_____
_____
_____
_____
_____
_____
_____
_____
_____
_____
_____

Day 67: Flourishing Tree

Devina H. Collier

Blessed is the man that trusteth in the Lord, and whose hope the Lord is. For he shall be as a tree planted by the waters, and that spreadeth out her roots by the river, and shall not see when heat cometh, but her leaf shall be green; and shall not be careful in the year of drought, neither shall cease from yielding fruit.
Jeremiah 17:7-8

The roots of trees go very deep, spreading beneath the ground, stable and secure. The branches of a tree, rooted in Jesus Christ, reach heavenward, yielding fruit every season and remaining unaffected by drought.

Doesn't that word picture create a longing to be firmly planted in the Lord; to be like a tree that flourishes no matter what comes?

Sisters, what has come into your life to stunt your growth? Is it fear, insecurity, or doubt?

Trust in the Lord and in His mighty power! He can and will accomplish every good thing for His purpose! You are a tree rooted in Him. The wind cannot blow you over. The sun cannot scorch your leaves. The drought cannot destroy your fruit.

Devina H. Collier

Arise, sisters, and be that tree planted by the river, beautiful and prosperous.

He shall be like a tree planted by the rivers of water, that brings forth its fruit in its season, whose leaf also shall not wither; and whatever he does shall prosper. Psalm 1:3

Today's exercise may be a little out of your comfort zone. Ask the Lord in prayer to help you be deeply planted in Him. Draw or paint a picture of a tree planted near a river. Show the tree's roots going deep into the ground. Draw leaves and fruit on the tree. Let this be a reminder that you are beautifully established in the Lord, able to withstand every season of drought.

Prayer:

_____

_____

_____

_____

_____

_____

_____

Tree with roots:
_____

Day 68: Our Father's Love

The Spirit itself beareth witness with our spirit, that we are the children of God. Romans 8:16

Daughters everywhere have longed for their fathers love and nurture. Striving to please their dads, girls often grow up insecure about their identity if their fathers were harsh, unloving, or absent.

My sisters, having received Christ, we are welcomed as daughters of God Most High. He is the most tender, loving Father a girl could have. Insecurity has no hold on us. We bear His name, and our security is found in Him.

The Father's love is unlike any affection we have ever received. It is unconditional and unchanging. God's love for us is not based on our performance. He does not withdraw His love when we do something wrong. No matter what, our heavenly Father nurtures us as His own.

Devina H. Collier

Today's exercise may be difficult for some. Find a quiet place to journal about your earthly father. Write down all the ways you tried to please him. Was he receptive to your love, or did you feel rejected? Read Psalm 68:5-6 and Romans 8:15. Write down the ways your Father in heaven loves you and cares for you.

Prayer and Action Steps:

_____
_____
_____
_____
_____
_____
_____
_____
_____
_____
_____
_____
_____
_____
_____
_____
_____
_____
_____
_____
_____
_____

Day 69: The Good Shepherd

The Lord is my shepherd; I shall not want. He maketh me to lie down in green pastures: He leadeth me beside the still waters. He restoreth my soul: He leadeth me in the path of righteousness for His name's sake.
Psalm 23:1-3

Deep in the heart of Italy, where herds of sheep are still abundant, a sheepdog called the s is trained to be a guardian of the lambs. From the time they are pups, these dogs are integrated into the herds and trained to protect the sheep from wolves. Rain or shine, these animals are devoted to guarding the flock at all cost.

Jesus is our Good Shepherd. He lays down His life for every lamb in the fold. He knows His sheep and His sheep know Him. (John 10:14-16)

In a world that doesn't feel safe and secure, we can be assured that our Good Shepherd guards us every step of the way. Even through rocky places, He is there, gently guiding us with His rod and staff. Lovingly, He leads us to green pastures

Devina H. Collier

where we find rest. He provides Living Water, that we might never thirst again. Jesus Christ is the Restorer of our souls.

Sisters, we don't have to worry about wolves when we remain close to the Shepherd. His path of righteousness is well guarded, eventually leading us to eternal life.

On YouTube, listen to this piano version of the old hymn "*Savior, like a Shepherd Lead Us.*" Let the words and music draw you to the green pasture of rest, knowing you have a good, good Shepherd.

What did the Lord speak to your heart?

_____

_____

_____

_____

_____

_____

_____

_____

_____

_____

_____

_____

_____

Devina H. Collier

Devina H. Collier

Day 70: The Relationship that sets us Free

And ye shall know the truth, and the truth shall make you free. John 8:32

Knowing God, *really knowing Him*, is much different than knowing *about* Him. Our relationship with the Lord is based on faith, not merely head-knowledge. So, how can a person be sure they are actually in a relationship with God?

My sisters, it's not about being able to describe Jesus or name facts about Him. It's about surrendering our lives to Him—the Way, the Truth, and the Life. And once we know the Truth, the Truth sets us free.

Free from what?

Free from every insecurity, every guilt, and every shame. An intimate relationship with the Savior liberates us. By His Spirit living in us, we *know*, without a doubt, that we have been forever set free.

Devina H. Collier

Sisters, do you know Him, *really* know Him? Do you love Him, *really* love Him?

Recommit your life to Jesus Christ today. No matter how long you've been a Christian, take some time to reconnect with the Savior. Cultivate your relationship by fellowshipping with Him in worship, learning more about Him through His word, and communing with Him in prayer.

What does it mean to you to be set free? Write a prayer of thanks. List 5-10 things about your freedom in Christ.

Prayer and Action Steps:

_____
_____
_____
_____
_____
_____
_____
_____
_____
_____
_____
_____
_____
_____
_____

Devina H. Collier

Rise and Shine

Pride
Day 71: Humility

*By humility and the fear of the Lord
Are riches and honor and life.
Proverbs 22:4*

There is no other name in the heavens above or the earth below, that deserves all glory, honor, and praise. There is power in the name of Jesus! And we are His people, women who bear His name. What an honor! What a privilege!

Pride has no place in the lives of those who are called by the name of Jesus. No place whatsoever. And there is only one remedy for pride—the humbling of oneself before the Maker of heaven and earth.

What a glorious sight it would be, if the nations humbled themselves before the Lord and turned from their ways. Can you imagine the outpouring of blessing?

My sisters, even if the world does not acknowledge the Creator, we must set the

Devina H. Collier

example. We, who are called by His name, must act justly, love mercy, and walk humbly with our God. (Micah 6:8)

Pray, seek Him, call out in humble praise and adoration. Turn from pride. And He will hear from heaven and be faithful and just to forgive.

Spend some extra time with the Lord today, in a lengthy time of prayer. Schedule an hour or more to fast, pray, and humble yourself before God. Commit to praying for our nation, its leaders, and the rest of the world, asking the Lord for mercy and thanking Him for His extended grace.

Prayer:

_____
_____
_____
_____
_____
_____
_____
_____
_____
_____
_____
_____

Rise and Shine

Devina H. Collier

Day 72: Fear Him and Live!

When pride comes, then comes shame;
But with the humble is wisdom.
Proverbs 11:2

What is the purpose of pride? When you stop to think about it, isn't pride a striving to be recognized as superior or more knowledgeable than others?

Pride tries to make others feel "less than." It is a stubbornness that will not yield or admit wrongdoing. But all it really does is bring shame. There is no wisdom in pride.

The fear of the Lord is the beginning of wisdom: and the knowledge of the holy is understanding. (Proverbs 9:10.) To fear God is to revere Him with the utmost honor and respect, recognizing ourselves as nothing before Him.

Humility opens the door of communication between us and the Lord. With an open and yielding spirit before God, we can hear what He has to say. Pride doesn't like to yield or be open to

Devina H. Collier

anyone. It prevents us from receiving life-giving wisdom.

Has Jesus been prompting you to make some changes, but you pridefully reject His leading? What part of your mind, body, heart, or spirit has been closed off to the Lord's wisdom? Is it your health, finances, a person or thing?

Let pride go. Ask Jesus to strip it off your mind (soul), body and spirit. List 3 action steps you can take to not allow pride to get a foothold.

Prayer and Action Steps:

_____
_____
_____
_____
_____
_____
_____
_____
_____
_____
_____
_____
_____
_____
_____

Day 73: Resistance

*God resisteth the proud, but giveth
grace unto the humble.
James 4:6*

It is true that God cannot look upon sin. It goes against His very nature of love, light, and holiness. Pride repels the Lord. It stands in opposition to Him. And He resists it at all cost.

For the believer in Christ, our sin doesn't change God's eternal love for us. However, our sin stands between us and the Lord. Like a partition that separates one room from another, sin gets in the way of our communion with Him. The good news is, we can, at any time, humble ourselves before the throne and watch that partition blow right over. Showers of mercy and grace are waiting for you. For "grace upon grace" is what the Lord gives to the humble. *And of his fulness have all we received, and grace for grace. (John 1:16)*

Isn't that beautiful?

Perhaps, you have allowed sin to interrupt your communion with God. Maybe, there is a root of pride that is standing in the way of receiving the fullness of His grace. Remember, He resists the proud, but gives grace to the humble. Let humility blow down every wall of resistance.

Do some resistance training today. Notice how each movement becomes a little harder as your muscles begin to get tired. In a spiritual sense, correlate the resistance you feel to any resistance you've had toward God. Let go of anything that is coming between you and the Lord. In prayer ask the Lord to help you tear down walls of resistance towards Him. Write 5-10 words that are opposite of resistance, such as liberation, peace, help and so on.

Prayer and Action Steps:

_____
_____
_____
_____
_____
_____
_____
_____
_____
_____

Devina H. Collier

Devina H. Collier

Day 74: False Beliefs and New Truths

Do not be wise in your own eyes; fear the Lord and depart from evil. It will be health to your flesh, and strength to your bones.
Proverbs 3:7-8

Have you ever believed something your whole life, only to grow up and realize it wasn't true? Perhaps, your grandmother taught you an old wives' tale that you thought was real. Or, you learned something at school that later proved to be false.

We base our choices off what we believe. We change our beliefs, we change our choices. We must always be willing to admit false beliefs and learn new truths. That's one of the beauties of God's Word. Each time we open it, He reveals something new and wonderful to us.

Being wise in our own eyes, because of our successes, achievements, degrees, or knowledge, can be a form of pride. Whatever wisdom we have gained is nothing compared to the wisdom of God.

The Lord gives us everything we need for *life and godliness*. *(2 Peter 1:3)* For our physical, spiritual, and emotional health, He provides the answers. Whatever beneficial things we have learned in life we can attribute to *Him—the Author and Perfecter of our faith. (Hebrews 12:1-3)*

Write down something you used to believe, but later found out wasn't true. Now, pray about your current beliefs. Is there anything that doesn't align with God's Word? Let go of any bit of wisdom that does not come from the mouth of the Lord.

Prayer and Action Steps:

_____

_____

_____

_____

_____

_____

_____

_____

_____

_____

_____

Rise and Shine

Devina H. Collier

Day 75: In Step with the Spirit

Better is the end of a thing than the beginning thereof: and the patient in spirit is better than the proud in spirit.
Ecclesiastes 7:8

You've probably heard the phrase, "Patience is a virtue." But for many of us, patience is more of a struggle than a virtue. Traffic jams, work, kids that won't cooperate, spouses that annoy us... so many things test our patience!

Often, we'd rather jump to the end of something then do what it takes to get there. If we want to lose weight, we look for the "quick fix" without looking for the root problems. If we want to make more money, we look for "get rich quick" strategies. We want instant results without being patient through diligence and hard work. This tells us not to despise humbled beginning.

The Christian life is all about patience. Waiting on God is an integral part of walking in step with His Spirit.

Devina H. Collier

If we live in the Spirit, let us also walk in the Spirit.
(Galatians 5:25)

Running ahead of God or lagging behind is really an exertion of pride. It says that "we know best." But when we make it our goal to do *nothing* outside of His leading, everything works out better than we could've imagined. His ways are always better than ours.

Spend 20-30 minutes on the treadmill or take a walk around the block. With each step, pray for the patience to remain in step with the Holy Spirit—not running ahead or lagging behind. List 5-10 words that line up with patience, such as endurance, strength and so on.

Prayer and Action Steps:

_____

_____

_____

_____

_____

_____

_____

_____

_____

_____

Purpose
Day 76: Keep on Keeping on

And we know that all things work together for good to them that love God, to them who are the called according to his purpose.
Romans 8:28

Today's verse is perhaps the most commonly quoted verse within Christian circles. We share it with those going through tough times. We remind ourselves of it when we are discouraged. And that is a good thing!

However, I'm afraid it's become so familiar to us, we have forgotten the magnitude of its meaning. The promise within Romans 8:28 is nothing short of remarkable! To KNOW that everything we face is going to work out for our good, is a blessed assurance that we cannot fully comprehend!

No matter what we face, God sees it. No matter what the struggle, God's got it. And we can fully trust Him to work it all out. What strength that gives us, my sisters! What motivation to "keep on keeping on!"

 Devina H. Collier

Do not give up. Wherever you are today, lift your chin in confidence—not confidence in self, but in the mighty working of God in your life. Not only will He work it out, He will work it out for your good.

Remember, it is not His will to hurt us or discourage us. It is His will to comfort and give us rest.

Come to Me, all you who labor and are heavy laden, and I will give you rest. Take My yoke upon you and learn from Me, for I am gentle and lowly in heart, and you will find rest for your souls. For My yoke is easy and My burden is light. (Matthew 11:28-30)

In prayer, thank God for giving you comfort and helping you to endure. Ask Him to anchor you and give comfort when burdens are pressing you. Tell Him to saturate your mind (soul), body and spirit with His yoke! Let it be a reminder that God is working everything out for your good. You can trust Him! List 5 words that are the opposite of yoke, such as break, loosen and so on.

Prayer and Action Steps:

_____
_____
_____
_____

Rise and Shine

Day 77: Alpha and Omega

*Declaring the end from the beginning,
and from ancient times things that are
not yet done, saying, 'My counsel shall
stand, and I will do all My pleasure.'*
Isaiah 46:10

Jesus declared that He is the Alpha and Omega, the beginning and the end. (Revelation 1:8) He is the same yesterday, today, and tomorrow. His purpose stands the test of all eternity, no matter what the seasons of the earth bring.

And so, it is with our lives. Times change, and things come and go, yet our purpose in Christ stands firm. On days when we feel like we have no purpose, it is the enemy trying to distract us from the vision God has placed in our hearts.

Do you know what your purpose is? What has the Lord spoken to your spirit? What is holding you back?

Devina H. Collier

Perhaps, you are like Moses, who argued against the Lord, insisting he could not be the Lord's mouthpiece.

Then Moses said to the Lord, "O my Lord, I am not eloquent, neither before nor since You have spoken to Your servant; but I am slow of speech and slow of tongue." Exodus 4:10

But God said this: *"Who has made man's mouth? Or who makes the mute, the deaf, the seeing, or the blind? Have not I, the Lord? Now therefore, go, and I will be with your mouth and teach you what you shall say." (Exodus 4:11-12)*

My sisters, do not be like Moses, who continued to argue with the Lord! Do not forsake His divine purpose for you. If He has called you, He will equip you with everything you need to carry out His will.

Petition the Lord. When He answers, write down everything He says and then pray for the strength to do it. (Remember, everything the Lord calls you to do will align with His Word.) Spend some time rediscovering your purpose. God's purpose for you is tied to your natural gifts and talents. For example, what motivates you? This could be your motivational gifts. What are you passionate about? Write it down and steps to take for you to walk in your calling.

Prayer and Action Steps:

_____
_____
_____
_____
_____
_____
_____
_____
_____
_____
_____
_____
_____
_____
_____
_____
_____
_____
_____
_____
_____
_____
_____
_____
_____
_____
_____

Devina H. Collier

Day 78: Seasons with a Purpose

*To every thing there is a season, and a time
to every purpose under the heaven.
Ecclesiastes 3:1*

Did you know that nothing escapes the Sovereignty of God? Not one sparrow falls to the ground unnoticed by the Master of the Universe. (Matthew 10:29-31)

Why, then, do bad things happen? That has been the age-old question—the one that has drawn many away from putting their faith in Christ. Yet, His ways are not our ways, nor our thoughts His thoughts.

For my thoughts are not your thoughts, neither are your ways my ways, saith the Lord. For as the heavens are higher than the earth, so are my ways higher than your ways, and my thoughts than your thoughts. Isaiah 55:8-9

Whatever hardship has blown into your life, there is assurance that God is sovereign. You can know that there is a higher purpose for the trial, that He has everything under control, and that He is aware of everything you're going through. Oh, how He loves you!

Try to see the ups-and-downs of life as "seasons with a purpose." Praise Him in the good times and bad. Trust that He is still on the throne and that He is working it all out for your ultimate good—according to His will.

Can I get an amen?

Sometimes there will be sunshine and rain, while other times there will be freezing temperatures and storms. In prayer, thank God for being walking you through the seasons of winter, spring, summer, and fall. Write 5 words that describe purpose, such as resolve, direction, ambition and so on.

Prayer and Action Steps:

_____

_____

_____

_____

_____

_____

_____

Day 79: Holy Calling

Who hath saved us, and called us with an holy calling, not according to our works, but according to his own purpose and grace, which was given us in Christ Jesus before the world began...
2 Timothy 1:9

Blessed is he who comes in the name of the Lord! (Psalm 118:26). We have been called with a holy calling, not because we've done anything to earn it, but because our God has graced us with a purpose that was ordained before the world began.

Isn't that awesome? My sisters, God have saved us by the blood of His own Son, that we would forsake the calling our flesh and embrace His holy calling!

Whatever we do outside of His will cannot prosper. Striving against the will of God is like running in circles and going nowhere.

Devina H. Collier

My sisters, let us surrender to the Lord's perfect plan. His way is so much better! He's had it in mind for all eternity, so that *in this day and age*, you would rise up and live it out. You have been called with a holy calling, to walk in faith for the glory of His kingdom!

And who knoweth whether thou art come to the kingdom for such a time as this? (Esther 4:14).

In prayer, thank God for blessing you and for placing on your life a holy calling. Write the words, "For such a time as this…" I was created to do, (then list it out!)

Prayer and Action Steps:

_____

_____

_____

_____

_____

_____

_____

_____

_____

_____

_____

_____

_____

_____

Day 80: Statement of Belief

*Fulfill ye my joy, that ye be likeminded,
having the same love, being of one
accord, of one mind.*
Philippians 2:2

The Bible is true when it says that where "two or more are gathered in His name, He is there." (Matthew 18:20) However, it can also be said that where two or more are gathered there is conflict!

People are people. Conflict will arise, even amongst believers. However, it is God's desire that we be of one accord. In fact, when Jesus prayed for us, He asked the Father to unify us as a testimony of the Savior.

That they all may be one; as thou, Father, art in Me, and I in thee, that they also may be one in us: that the world may believe that thou hast sent Me. (John 17:2).

Sisters, the world needs to see us stand in agreement. When we fight and argue among ourselves, our Christian testimony is tarnished. This

Devina H. Collier

doesn't mean we can't have healthy disagreements, but it does indicate the importance of being unified in the essentials of the faith.

Are you secure in the foundational truths of the Bible? Are you certain about what you believe? In what areas would you like to learn more?

Every one of us has areas in which we need to grow. We won't know everything until we reach heaven! It is OK to continue to study and learn about God. It's even OK to tell someone you don't have the answer! But always be willing to expand your learning.

Today, write out your own belief statement. In your personal statement, include what you believe about God, the Bible, Salvation, and whatever else you feel the need to write. If you have trouble defining your beliefs, reach out to a trusted pastor or Bible teacher for help. Most of all, search the Scriptures to solidify what you believe and why you believe it.

Prayer and Action Steps:

_____

_____

_____

Devina H. Collier

Trust
Day 81: Trust in the Unknown

*Trust in the Lord with all thine heart; and
lean not unto thine own understanding.
In all thy ways acknowledge him,
And he shall direct thy paths.*
Proverbs 3:5-6

Have you ever been at a crossroads in life, needing to make a critical choice? Perhaps, both ways seemed good to you, but you just weren't sure what to do.

This life is full of decisions that need to be made, and often we feel unsure about making them. Past mistakes cause us to doubt our judgment and worries about the future cause uncertainty. However, God cares about every decision we make—big or small. He knows the exact route we should take in every circumstance. Taking the time to acknowledge the Lord, and ask for direction, is always the right decision.

Now, He may ask us to move forward without knowing all the details, but that's OK. Like

Abraham, who was called out of his country and into the unknown, God sometimes calls us to go into unknown territory.

Now the Lord had said to Abram: Get out of your country, from your family and from your father's house, to a land that I will show you. I will make you a great nation; I will bless you.. Genesis 12:1-2

Without full trust in the Lord, Abram would have argued with God. He would have hesitated and perhaps even ignored the Lord's leading. But faithfully he went.

My sisters, do we have that kind of trust? Are we ready to step into the unknown? Or do we need to see every detail before we move forward? Walk by faith!

If the Lord is asking you to step into the unknown, it is for a mighty purpose. Marvel at the ways God works and put your trust fully in Him today.

Search Google for a map of Abraham and Sarah's journeys. As God led them from place to place, He was working out His divine purpose for them. The end goal was to bless Abraham and build an entire nation from his seed. In prayer ask the Lord to take any blinders off your eyes and for the Holy

Spirit to lead you. List the things you sense Jesus asking you to do and any step to take.

Prayer and Action Steps:

_____

_____

_____

_____

_____

_____

_____

_____

_____

_____

_____

_____

_____

_____

_____

_____

_____

_____

_____

_____

_____

_____

_____

_____

_____

Devina H. Collier

Day 82: With You in the Fiery Furnace

When thou passest through the waters, I will be with thee; and through the rivers, they shall not overflow thee: when thou walkest through the fire, thou shalt not be burned; neither shall the flame kindle upon thee.
Isaiah 43:2

One of the most amazing accounts of trust in the Bible, is the account of Shadrach, Meshach, and Abednego in the fiery furnace. The Old Testament story in the book of Daniel, tells of three upstanding young men who would not bow down to the golden statue King Nebuchadnezzar had erected. Because of their faithfulness to God, they were sentenced to be thrown into a fiery furnace.

The most remarkable part of their story was what they said to the king:

"...our God whom we serve is able to deliver us from the burning fiery furnace, and He will deliver us from your hand, O king. But if not, let it be known to you, O king, that we do not serve your gods, nor

will we worship the gold image which you have set up." (Daniel 3:17-18)

What steadfast and incredible trust they had in God!

And you know what? The Lord entered that furnace with them. For as the king looked into the flames, he saw not three men, but four—One of them that looked like the Son of God. When King Nebuchadnezzar commanded them to come out, not one hair on their heads was scorched, nor was there any smell of smoke on them.

My sisters, what a mighty God we serve! He walks amidst the flames with us. He passes through waters that threaten to overflow us.

During your quiet time, light a candle and reflect on Psalm 66:8-12 and Isaiah 43:2. Know that in every fiery trial, God is in the midst of it with you. In prayer, thank God for walking with you through the trials of life. List 5 trials, He walked you through.

Prayer and Action Steps:

_____

_____

_____

_____

Devina H. Collier

Day 83: Lovingkindness in the Morning

Cause me to hear Your lovingkindness in the morning, for in You do I trust; Cause me to know the way in which I should walk, For I lift up my soul to You.
Psalm 143:8

Do you wake up in the morning eager to hear from the Lord? Or, do you wake up with a feeling of dread, wishing you could stay in bed? Sometimes, thoughts of the day's responsibilities come flooding in, and we wish we didn't have to face the day.

My sisters, let the lovingkindness of the Lord be the first thing you hear in the morning. He is singing over you! *The Lord thy God in the midst of thee is mighty; he will save, he will rejoice over thee with joy; he will rest in his love, he will joy over thee with singing. (Zephaniah 3:17)*

As you stretch, reach out in praise to the God of fresh starts and new mercies. As you wipe the sleep from your eyes, pray for vision that sees the ways of the Lord. And as you rise, seek His loving kindness and wait for His gentle voice to lead you. The day-to-day grind doesn't have to be depressing. We don't have to wake up every day with a sense of dread. Everything we do can be done with joy when we start out by hearing the tender voice of our loving Father.

Colossians 3:23 reminds us that *"in all the work you are doing, work the best you can, as unto the Lord and not men."*

With that perspective, our tasks of the day become opportunities instead of obligations. Will you pray for a new perspective? Will you listen for the voice of the Lord as you awaken to a new day?

Begin making your "to-do" list before you go to bed at night. By writing down the next day's responsibilities, you'll get them out of your head and be able to sleep better. Then, when you wake up, you'll know that your tasks are already on paper, and you'll be able to focus on the voice of the Lord first.

Prayer and Action Steps:

_____

_____

 Devina H. Collier

Day 84: The Fastest way to Peace

*Whenever I am afraid, I will trust in You. In
God (I will praise His word), in God I
have put my trust; I will not fear.
What can flesh do to me?
Psalm 56:3-4*

There are times when genuine fear grips our hearts, especially when a loved one is in harm's way. That kind of fear comes without warning and alerts us that something is wrong. However, the Bible says that even in genuine fear, we can still choose to trust God and praise Him in the midst of it.

The fastest way to peace is to declare the Word and raise hands of praise. Does that sound like an impossibility when fear sweeps in?

My sisters, no matter what comes our way, when we are willing to let go of mind-gripping fear to recite His Word and praise Him, the peace that passes understanding will come. And as impossible as it may seem, we can even offer thanks to God in that very circumstance.

...but in everything by prayer and supplication with thanksgiving let your requests be made known unto God. And the peace of God, which passeth all understanding, shall keep your hearts and minds through Christ Jesus. (Philippians 4:6-7)

Praying to God with thanksgiving in our hearts, even in the worst of times, is an act of trust. It shows the Lord that even though we are afraid, we trust Him.

In what areas do you struggle to trust God? Offer your fear to Him today. In the midst of fear, lift up hands of thanksgiving and release it to the Lord. Allow His peace to overcome you as you trust that He's got you and He's got your circumstance. In prayer ask the Lord to help you. List areas you struggle with and any action steps you can take that can help you.

Prayer and Action Steps:

_____
_____
_____
_____
_____

 Devina H. Collier

Day 85: The Shadow of the Almighty

He that dwelleth in the secret place of the most High shall abide under the shadow of the Almighty. I will say of the Lord, He is my refuge and my fortress: my God; in him will I trust.
Psalm 91:1-2

If you've ever been in the path of an intense storm, you've probably sensed the panic all around. People flood to the grocery store to stock up on supplies. Business owners board up their windows. And the news headlines make their predictions of how bad it is going to get. The most important thing during a storm is to find adequate shelter.

Our souls, as well, need shelter from the onslaught of the enemy. For he rushes in like a storm and bombards us with lies, worries, and temptations. However, we have a secret shelter, a shelter that stands against every storm. Under the shadow of Almighty God, our souls take refuge.

Devina H. Collier

The tried-and-true answer for the enemy is, "God is my fortress. In Him I put my trust." And you know what? At that moment, the devil has to flee. For in the name of Jesus, he no longer has a leg to stand on.

A fortress is heavily guarded. It is fortified and impenetrable. And the Lord God Almighty is that rampart for us. Sisters, do you believe that today? Are you running to the refuge of the shadow of the Most High, or are you exposing yourself to the enemy? Take cover today in God's presence. Healing is there!

Look up the words *refuge* and *fortress* in the dictionary and thesaurus? Write down the definitions that best describe how God protects you from the enemy. Thank Him for allowing you to abide under the shadow of His wings.

Prayer and Action Steps:

_____
_____
_____
_____
_____
_____
_____
_____

 Devina H. Collier

Faith
Day 86: The Final Exam

Wherefore the law was our schoolmaster to bring us unto Christ, that we might be justified by faith. But after that faith is come, we are no longer under a schoolmaster.
Galatians 3:24-25

"Faith" has become a label that the world gives to anyone who claims to have religion. Many who have head-knowledge of religious customs or traditions are considered people of faith. But true faith, as declared in the Word of God, is being sure of what we hope for and certain of what we do not see.

Now faith is the substance of things hoped for, the evidence of things not seen. (Hebrews 11:1)

Every bit of wisdom and knowledge that leads to putting faith in Jesus Christ, is like a "study guide," leading to the final exam—the testing of our hearts. For once our eyes are opened, faith replaces our head-knowledge and we become women of true faith.

Devina H. Collier

My sisters, are you considered "religious," or are you known as women of faith in Jesus Christ? Don't let religiosity define you. Be ready to give an answer to everyone who asks about your beliefs.

But sanctify the Lord God in your hearts: and be ready always to give an answer to every man that asketh you a reason of the hope that is in you with meekness and fear. (1 Peter 3:15)

Go back to school today, by making a list of things you were taught about God before you gave your life to Christ. Can you see how those teachings ultimately brought you to the Savior? Thank the Lord for planting seeds of faith in your heart and for sending His Son to turn your religion into the true faith. In prayer, thank God for uncovering what you could not see and revealing truth. List 5 ways the Lord has been faithful to you.

Prayer and Action Steps:

_____
_____
_____
_____
_____
_____
_____

Devina H. Collier

Day 87: Hold Back the Tidal Wave

For whatsoever is born of God overcometh the world: and this is the victory that overcometh the world, even our faith. Who is he that overcometh the world, but he that believeth that Jesus is the Son of God?
1 John 5:4-5

As Christians, we know that Jesus has overcome the world. But for us, living in the middle of the "mess," it can feel like the world has overcome us. Surrounded by sin and darkness that seems to be growing stronger each day, the massive tide of evil can cause us to waver.

But ladies, not only has Jesus overcome the world, WE have overcome the world. Belief in the Son of God is powerful enough to hold back the massive tidal wave of the world's influence.

Jesus prayed for His disciples, that they would live *in* the world but not be part *of* the world:

I pray not that thou shouldest take them out of the world, but that thou shouldest keep them from the evil. They are not of the world, even as I am not of the world. (John 17:15-16)

My sisters, for now, this is our temporary dwelling. We cannot pack up and move to another planet. However, we can and should live with our true home in mind. All the evil around us may seem insurmountable, but it cannot stand against faith in Jesus Christ. Declare that today!

 When you feel overwhelmed by the waves of the world's sin, declare these truths and stand firm in your faith:

- I believe in Jesus Christ, the Son of God!
- I am born of God, not the world!
- Jesus has overcome the world!
- I have overcome the world!

In prayer, let God know that He is your confidence. Then write 5 words related to conquer, such as triumph, prevail, and so on.

Prayer and Action Steps:

_____
_____
_____
_____

Day 88: One Touch of the Savior

And suddenly, a woman who had a flow of blood for twelve years came from behind and touched the hem of His garment. For she said to herself, "If only I may touch His garment, I shall be made well." But Jesus turned around, and when He saw her He said, "Be of good cheer, daughter; your faith has made you well." And the woman was made well from that hour.
Matthew 9:20-22

Twelve years is a long time, my sisters. The woman with the issue of blood, an unexplained illness that had isolated her and used up all the resources she had, held on to one last hope—the Savior's healing touch.

The sweet part about the story is that she didn't even expect to meet Him. She wanted nothing more than to touch the hem of his robe. What beautiful faith she had! And in one moment, twelve years of suffering were wiped away, healed and restored by the Savior's touch. Jesus said her faith has made her well. Faith is 100% confidence and trust in Jesus.

Devina H. Collier

Sisters, are you in need of the healing power of Jesus? Have you exhausted all other means? Do you feel isolated and forgotten? Contact me today, nevertheless for a health and wellness consultation.

Take heart! Be of good cheer! One touch from the Savior, and you will be healed!

More precious than gold is your faith. He knows your condition. And He is mighty to heal. Do you believe? Like the woman who thought, *If only I may touch His garment, I shall be made well*, do you believe that Jesus will heal you?

Find or purchase a small piece of fabric and hand-stitch a hem along one edge. Let every stitch be a declaration of faith, that even by the hem of His robe, Jesus is mighty to save! Let this exercise be an act of worship and faith that the Lord will make you well. In prayer ask the Lord to heal you. List some action steps to start living healthier.

Prayer and Action Steps:

_____
_____
_____
_____
_____

Devina H. Collier

Day 89: Only You Can Name Your Mountain

For verily I say unto you, That whosoever shall say unto this mountain, Be thou removed, and be thou cast into the sea; and shall not doubt in his heart, but shall believe that those things which he saith shall come to pass; he shall have whatsoever he saith. Therefore I say unto you, What things soever ye desire, when ye pray, believe that ye receive them, and ye shall have them.
Mark 11:23-24

Faith that can move mountains sounds like an exorbitant amount of faith, doesn't it? Such confidence! Yet Jesus said that it would only take faith as small as a mustard seed to move mountains. (Matthew 17:20)

What mountains need to be moved in your life? Anxiety, depression, addiction, or unbelief? Only you can name your mountain. But no matter how high, how wide, or how immovable it might seem, nothing is impossible with Christ.

In His name, and in His power, mountains crumble. The big question is, do we really desire for our mountains to be removed? Or, have we become accustomed to them?

Whatever things you desire, when you pray in belief and confidence, you shall have them. According to the will of the Father, anything that is in alignment with His will, you shall receive. And of course, He wants our mountains of affliction to be removed!

My sisters, with faith in Jesus Christ, faith as tiny as a seed, say to your mountain, "Be ye removed!" And watch it crumble before your very eyes.

In prayer, thank God for moving your mountain in advance. Draw the shape of a mountain. Now, write the name of that mountain across it. Be honest with yourself and honest with God. Put a name to your mountain and in faith, cast it into the depths of the sea.

Prayer and Action Steps:

_____
_____
_____
_____
_____
_____

Devina H. Collier

Mountain: _____

Day 90: Beautiful Witness of Light

But thou, O man of God, flee these things; and follow after righteousness, godliness, faith, love, patience, meekness. Fight the good fight of faith, lay hold on eternal life, to which you were also called and have confessed the good confession in the presence of many witnesses.
1 Timothy 6:11-12

Faith is a fight. It's a fight for all that is righteous. It is a good fight, but a battle nonetheless.

Those around us, who know that we are women of faith, are watching to see how we live our lives. How are we spending our time? How are we handling conflict? Are we walking in integrity?

Ladies, this doesn't mean we have to be perfect, or feel like we are performing. It does, however, mean that we allow our faith to shine through everything we do. It means we don't shy away from our beliefs. We don't hide the light of Jesus. Instead, we put it on a stand for all the world to see.

Devina H. Collier

No one, when he has lit a lamp, puts it in a secret place or under a basket, but on a lamp stand, that those who come in may see the light. (Luke 11:33)

Do others see the light of faith in you? Do they see you following after righteousness, godliness, and love? Sisters, remove the cover from your lamp and place it front-and-center! Let everyone in your sphere of influence see the light of Jesus in you! Fight the good fight of faith and cling to the eternal life promised by the Savior.

What a beautiful witness of light you are!

Visit an antique shop or boutique and look at all the unique lamps for sale. Consider purchasing one to place in a prominent place in your home as a reminder of the light you are to those around you. Ask the Lord to remind you to be a light even when things get tough. Write 5 words that represent a light, such as vivid, radiant and so on.

Prayer and Action Steps:

_____

_____

_____

_____

_____

Devina H. Collier

Rise and Shine

PART 2: Physical Healing!

POEM: He Answers Every Prayer

By Angela Washington

I knew I had a need,
God already made away.
Before I opened my mouth,
He had foreseen that I would pray.
He knew the words that I would speak,
before I started my request.
He knew the scripture I would read,
before my body would start to rest.
It is amazing what God knows,
and how He answers every prayer.
Forever with me when I'm needy,
I am grateful He hears my prayers.

The Lord Provides Everything You Need to Heal

Behold, I will bring it health and cure, and I will cure them, and will reveal unto them the abundance of peace and truth.
Jeremiah 33:6

And Jesus, moved with compassion, put forth his hand, and touched him, and saith unto him, I will; be thou clean.
Mark 1:41

Many are the afflictions of the righteous: but the LORD delivereth him out of them all.
Psalm 34:19

...the fruit thereof shall be for meat, and the leaf thereof for medicine.
Ezekiel 47:12

Devina H. Collier

26 Medicinal Purposes of Holy Basil: The King of Herbs

The compounds in Basil (*Ocimum sanctum or Tulsi*), can heal many health conditions and aid in the promotion of good health. Basil is majorly used as a seasoning agent in our food, but most are unaware of the history and medicinal benefits of the plant. Thousands of scientific researchers and clinical trials have proven the beneficial aspect of Basil. Its use has been predominant since centuries in different parts of the Mediterranean, like Asia, and especially India, where it is renowned for its medicinal properties. Researchers have proven the healing properties of basil are stronger than most of the modern medications combined, and without question, basil can improve health.

Proven benefits:

1. Basil has antifungal effects which helps to act against fungal infections like *Candida Albicans*.[1]
2. The botanical from Basil, in the form of aerosol has a potent anti-mosquito effect, thus proving its anti-microbial effects.[2]
3. Basil helps to eliminate mosquito larvae and thus helps in controlling the mosquito

population, especially in places where mosquitoes are a major health issue.[3] [4]

4. Basil has an insulin like action thus having anti-diabetic properties and have helped in regulating blood glucose levels.[5]

5. This botanical also has proven to have antibiotic properties acting against different bacteria and thus reducing infection.[6]

6. Basil has potent anti-viral effects. Research shows that it can act against a wide variety of viruses like Herpes simplex virus Types 1 and 2, and Hepatitis B virus.[7]

7. Basil has anti-protozoal actions which acts against detrimental protozoa (parasites) such as trypanosome (transmitted by flies, ticks, and leeches), guardian (from eating or drinking liquids that are contaminated with infected feces), and Trichomonas (STD).[8]

8. Basil acts against the organism causing malaria (Plasmodium) thus having anti-malarial properties.[9]

9. Extracts of Basil have shown to act against different helminths (parasites) in the human body.[10]

10. Basil has potent antioxidant properties.[11]

11. Basil helps against high blood pressure, thus having anti-hypertensive properties.[12]
12. Basil helps to keep the cerebral neurons active and thus enhances memory and protects against disorders like Alzheimer's, and dementia.[13]
13. The botanical also helps in reduction of stress and calming the mind.[14]
14. Sweet Basil has shown to act against arthritis and help the swelling and reduce the pain and delay the onset.[15]
15. It helps to fight against diarrhea and other gastrointestinal infections.[16]
16. In a mice study, Basil helped protect their body from different agents that leads to cancer thus having anti-carcinogenic properties.[17]
17. Basil supports the reduction of respiratory disorders.[18]
18. It helps in the healing process of cough and cold. [18]
19. It also helps to reduce emesis or vomiting.[19]
20. Increases immunity, thus strengthening the body against different microorganism and diseases.[20]
21. Basil acts against allergies by reducing inflammation in the tissues.[21]

22. Basil helps to reduce fever by reducing the temperature of the body, thus having an anti-pyretic effect.[22]
23. It also helps in healing of ulcers and having a soothing effect on them.[23]
24. Basil extracts have shown to provide protection against the injurious agents that harm the liver, for example fats, alcohol, and medications.[24]
25. Other properties of the botanical are radioprotection, anti-cataract, analgesic, cardio protection etc.[25]

~ Recover Me ~

Then shall thy light break forth as the morning, and thine health shall spring forth speedily: and thy righteousness shall go before thee; the glory of the Lord shall be thy reward. Isaiah 58:8

18 Medicinal Purposes of Garlic: The Gate Keeper

Not only is Garlic mentioned in Numbers 11:5 in the Holy Bible in as a favorite food and spice of the Egyptians and the Israelites, but also, has been proven throughout history in ancient civilizations to have strong medicinal properties. It's no wonder why Babylon, China, Greece, Rome, and India love it because one or two cloves everyday can reduce the risk of major chronic diseases.

The medicinal effects have been proven in hundreds of clinical trials. Garlic belongs to the Allium family and the bulb which grows underground is the main source of the botanic. The sulfurous compound Allicin is the constituent which facilitates health benefits. An added advantage of Garlic is that it has more benefits than side effects, although it has been reported to thin the blood, which is not a bad thing when a person has venous congestion (congested bloodstream) or thick blood. Pharmaceuticals use medications like coumadin and warfarin to thin the blood against blood clots.

Some of the major health benefits of Garlic are:

1. It increases endurance to work and exercise by acting as an anti-fatigue agent.[26]
2. It has a very nutritive composition consisting of a variety of essential nutrients like Vitamin B6, B12, iron, phosphorous, and manganese. These ingredients are the building blocks of our body and contribute to several important functions.[27]
3. Researchers have found out that Garlic helps in giving protection against dementia and Alzheimer's.[28]
4. Garlic not only helps in giving protection against cold, but also helps in minimizing it.[29]
5. Garlic has an anti-microbial effect, i.e. It acts against various disease-causing organisms. Studies have also revealed that Garlic was successful in eliminating microorganisms which was resistant to major modern day anti-biotic.[30]
6. Garlic helps in balancing blood glucose levels, thus helping in the management of treatment of diabetes.[31]
7. Garlic also helps in increasing immunity, thus making the body stronger and resistant to pathogens.[32]
8. Researchers have found Garlic provides protection against different types of

cancers like brain, colon, prostate, breast, bladder, skin etc.[33]

9. Garlic helps in elimination of heavy metal accumulation out of the body, thus aiding in detoxification.[34]

10. Garlic helps in maintaining bone function and bone health in osteoarthritis.[35]

11. Garlic helps in lowering cholesterol and triglycerides.[36]

12. It helps in decreasing body fat and managing obesity.[37]

13. It helps in balancing blood pressure in hypertensive individuals.[38]

14. Garlic helps in protecting the liver from chemical injury caused by medications, chemicals and toxins.[39]

15. Garlic has anti-fungal properties and researchers have shown that it has the ability to reduce thrush among infants.[40]

16. It acts against viruses like herpes, influenza, rhinovirus, and cytomegalovirus.[41]

17. Researcher found Garlic helps inhibit and reduce atherosclerosis – which is a disease where a thick layer of fat is deposited in the arteries and veins which can lead to blockage, heart attack or stroke.[42]

18. Researchers found Garlic helped reduce growth rates of cancer cells by blocking the G2/M phase. It was Garlic's allylsulfide derivatives and other potent compounds that blocked it.[43]

~ Life and Health ~

My son, attend to my words; incline thine ear unto my sayings. Let them not depart from thine eyes; keep them in the midst of thine heart. For they are life unto those that find them, and health to all their flesh. Proverbs 4:20-22

20 Medicinal Purposes of Ginger: The Defender

Ginger (*Zingiber officinale*) is a popular spice. Apart from its use in food, its medicinal benefits are innumerable. Gingerol is the main ingredient in Ginger that is the potent medicinal property. The nutritional content of Ginger can provide the human body with a variety of nutrients that are necessary for the development of organs.

There have been thousands of researches and clinical trials done all over the world which proves that Ginger is one of the best herbs for many ailments.

A few of the most important health benefits of the botanic are:

1. Anti-bacterial properties that defend the body against infectious bacteria such as the Pseudomonas that causes pneumonia and other infections of the bone, blood and urinary system. That bacteria are resistant to many antibiotics.[44] [45]
2. Ginger's anti-inflammatory properties help to decrease inflammation caused by various insect bite, and physical injuries.[46]

3. Fighting cold and flu is one of the most common uses of this botanic. Traditionally it is consumed as a tea for throat problems.[47]
4. The botanic analgesic properties help to reduce pain as well.[48]
5. Ginger also has anti-emetic properties, it helps to reduce nausea and vomiting because of its pungent constituents.[49]
6. The botanic also helps in reducing morning sickness in pregnancy.[50]
7. Ginger helps in digestion and decreasing stomach discomfort.[51]
8. Ginger helps regulate skin problems like allergic dermatitis.[52]
9. Due to its soothing and anti-inflammatory and anti-allergic effects, Ginger helps in the management of asthma and respiratory tract discomforts.[53]
10. The botanic also protects against hepatotoxicity (liver toxicity).[54]
11. Researchers have found that Ginger is helpful in fighting against cancerous tumor cells by acting against them.[55]
12. It helps in protecting DNA from damages, as well as act against genetic disorders.[56]
13. Ginger helps to balance blood pressure and aids in hypertension.[57]

14. Ginger lowers cholesterol and triglycerides.[58]
15. Ginger has properties that help regulate metabolism and support the management of obesity.[59]
16. Different clinical trials have revealed that Ginger helps in the control of Type 2 diabetes. [60]
17. The botanic helps in fighting Non-Alcoholic Fatty Liver disease by protecting the liver from agents like high fats (elevated cholesterol).[61]
18. Ginger also has anti-ulcer properties.[62]
19. Ginger is a potent anti-viral agent, especially against respiratory viruses.[63]
20. Clinical research revealed that the botanic has strong anti-fungal properties and acts well against candida infections.[64]

~ Mercy Everlasting ~

...Bless the LORD, all his works in all places of his dominion: bless the LORD, O my soul. Psalm 103:22

19 Medicinal Purposes of Cinnamon: The Balancer

Cinnamon is one of the most commonly used herbs around the world. Its use is prevalent both in the modern era and the ancient times. The herb is not only filled with flavors but also with natural compounds which have potent health benefits. Researchers throughout the world have provided thousands of clinical trials.

Some of the most important benefits of the herb are:

1. Cinnamon is best known for the management of Type 2 diabetes by balancing blood glucose levels and by modulating transport of glucose in the body.[65]
2. Clinical research has revealed that Cinnamon supports the antioxidant status of the body and protect against oxidative injury.[66]
3. Controls cholesterol and other lipids - studies have shown that Cinnamon decreases the level of triglyceride, bad cholesterol (LDL), and the total cholesterol.[67]

4. Helps in weight loss. The herb's action against lipid and on metabolism, helps in reducing excess weight. [68]

5. Cinnamon is anti-inflammatory by acting against inflammation. It's shown to help regulate inflammation response and promote quicker healing and recovery processes.[69]

6. Researchers have shown Cinnamon has anti-bacterial activities. It acts against many species of bacteria causing infections, thus helping to protect the body.[70]

7. It supports symptoms of Alzheimer's by helping to protect the brain and its neurons against age related degenerative changes.[71]

8. Cinnamon has analgesic actions. It is a potent botanic against pain and helps to relieve mild to moderate pain. [72]

9. It was found to support Pre-Menstrual Symptom. It helped reduce menstrual spasm and pain.[73]

10. Cinnamon supports poly cystic ovarian syndrome. It helps regulate the menstrual cycle and lessened severe symptoms of PCOS.[74]

11. The botanic is anti-fungal. Cinnamon helps to act against fungal microorganism and decrease fungal infections.[75]

12. Cinnamon helps to regulate mood and balance anxiety. [76]

13. It is a sect repellant. The strong smell of the herb helps to repel insects.[77]

14. Researchers have found Cinnamon to fight cancer. It acted against oxidative cellular damage and inhibited nuclear changes in the cell and reduced the formation and growth of cancerous cells.[78]

15. Cinnamon helps in the reduction of dental pain and inhibits dental decay.[79]

16. It protects cardio. The botanic helps to defend the heart and its functions, especially by decreasing atherosclerotic plaque lipids.[80]

17. It can be used as a mouth freshener, and anti-bacterial because it has shown to kill germs of the mouth.[81]

18. Cinnamon keeps skin healthy by maintaining optimal amounts of collagen in the skin, thus reducing age related changes.[82]

19. In rats, researchers have found out in clinical trials that Cinnamon protected their

liver from a variety of injurious agents and oxidative stress.[83]

~ Above All ~

Beloved, I wish above all things that thou mayest prosper and be in health, even as thy soul prospereth. 3 John 1:2

Devina H. Collier

18 Medicinal Purposes of Lavender: The Way Maker

Lavender (*Lavandula*) is from the mint family. It is an ancient herb originating from Europe, Asia and Africa. It has been used for thousands of years by our ancestors. Lavender oil is well known for its potent health benefits. The soothing scent of this herb helps to calm the mind and heal the body of anxiety and other ailments. It is one of the safest herbs.

1. Lavender not only soothes normal to mild headache, but also migraines due to its calming aroma.[84]
2. The components in the extracts of lavender helps to reduce depression.[85]
3. Lavender helps with insomnia by minimizing the symptoms of stress and making it easier to fall asleep and manage insomnia better.[86]
4. Studies in workplaces have found out that lavender essential oils can reduce anxiety.[87]
5. It has anti-microbial properties. The extracts have shown in research to act against various types of fungal microorganism at

the cellular level thus protecting the human body.[88]

6. It's helpful for eczema. There has been reports of many case studies where lavender extracts have helped heal different skin conditions, not just eczema.[89]

7. Lavender supports digestion. The flower and its extracts are well known for its gastric soothing properties. It helps to create a balance between the good and bad bacterium of the gastrointestinal system and promote proper digestion.[90]

8. It soothes acne. Acne is a common skin problem especially among young adults. Lavender acts as an emolument and a soother for acne.[91]

9. Lavender is anti-bacterial. Its potent botanic act against many types of bacterial and helps decrease infections. [92]

10. It is used for wound repair and healing. Lavender helps increase activity of fibroblast which helps in wound repair. Different research has shown that wounds tend to heal faster with the application of lavender.[93]

11. Lavender is one of the most beneficial essential oil in support and balance of diabetes.[94]
12. Lavender is analgesic. It helps in reduction in pain. Researchers have found the effects of Lavender decreases the pain and discomfort associated with dysmenorrhea.[95]
13. Lavender has shown to reduce respiratory congestion due to severe respiratory problems. Also cough, bronchitis, and sinusitis.[96]
14. Researchers have found the high content of antioxidants in Lavender helps in protecting the body against cancer. It also showed to protect the body from different health problems that might arise in a cancer patient for example immunity to normal cough and cold.[97]
15. In a mice study, researchers found lavender promoted hair growth in mice. Today, lavender is very popular for its effect on hair growth, hair health and its action against dandruff. It protects the hair from damage and supports overall good hair health. [98]

16. Studies have shown that lavender helps to maintain good cardiovascular health. It helps increase coronary circulation.[99]
17. It's anti-septic. The extract inhibits infectious growth of microorganism.[100]
18. Lavender has been shown to support the nervous system. Research studies have revealed that lavender has properties that protect against Alzheimer's disease, thus having neuroprotective, and antioxidant properties.[101]

~ Breath of Life ~

The spirit of God hath made me, and the breath of the Almighty hath given me life. Job 33:4

Devina H. Collier

16 Medicinal Purposes of Cayenne Pepper: The Enforcer

Cayenne pepper (capsaicin) is a hot and spicy herb that is a member of the chili pepper family which originated from South America. Apart from the fact that it is extremely flavorful when added to food, its medicinal properties are also noteworthy. Its high content of nutrients and antioxidants make it one of the best herbs to maintain overall health. Researchers have studied the effect of this botanic in thousands of clinical trials in both man and animals and the results are revolutionary.

Some of the most important uses of cayenne pepper are:

1. It has been shown to reduce damage to heart muscle by a heart attack. In recent years, researchers have found in animal trials that capsaicin has the ability to reduce pain and provide protection to the cardiac muscles in heart attacks. Also, a human clinical trial revealed that the botanic reduced the chance of cardiac cell death by 81%.[102]

2. It increases metabolism by helping to increase the production of heat in the body.[103]
3. It also helps with hypothermic (hypothermia) conditions because it increases body temperature.[104]
4. It is anti-obesity and reduces body weight by speeding up energy in cellular metabolism.[105]
5. Cayenne decreases nasal congestion due to it speeding up metabolism, which then acts on reducing mucous consistency.[106]
6. Studies show Cayenne improves psoriasis and helps the quality skin.[107]
7. Research shows Cayenne pepper helps balance blood glucose and is beneficial for Type 2 Diabetes.[108]
8. Cayenne pepper is commonly known for its effect on the cardiovascular system. The botanic especially helps to balance blood pressure.[109]
9. In animal studies, Cayenne helped decrease blood clots, maintained blood flow and good vascular function.[110]
10. Cayenne has been shown to balance cholesterol by helping to break down lipids, fats and triglycerides. Several animal studies

have provided evidence about the effects of Cayenne pepper on cholesterol.[111]

11. Cayenne pepper significantly desensitizes pain sensation in cluster headaches.[112]

12. It helps decrease high stomach acid production and gastritis.[113]

13. Cayenne pepper has botanical properties that help reduce neuralgia, and fibromyalgia pain.[114]

14. It has been discovered to help with pain after surgery.[115]

15. A researcher, Young-Joon Surh with The Journal of The National Cancer Institute reported that Cayenne pepper has special anti-cancer properties, which *"induced apoptosis in cultured cells derived from human cutaneous squamous cell carcinoma."* [116] [117]

16. Cayenne pepper consists of very high amounts of antioxidants, which acts against free radicals, or oxidative stress in cell, thus protecting the body from oxidative damage.[118]

~ Enduring Strength ~

I will love thee, O LORD, my strength. The LORD is my rock, and my fortress, and my deliverer; my God, my strength, in whom I will trust; my buckler, and the horn of my salvation, and my high tower.
Psalm 18:1-2

Devina H. Collier

18 Medicinal Purposes of Rosemary: The Unblocker

Rosemary (Rosmarinus officinalis) is a very common herb that we use in many cuisines throughout the world. Seldom is known about the medicinal qualities of this herb. It is highly nutritious and helps to support overall health. Rosemary extract has a variety of compounds, but the most potent ones are carnosic acid and rosmarinic acid.

The medicinal benefits are:

1. Helping with blood flow and optimal circulation. In a clinical study it inhibited thrombosis (blood clot).[119]
2. It's anti-bacterial. The botanic is widely used as a natural antibiotic for its strong action against bacterial microorganisms.[120]
3. The oil extract is soothing and has shown to reduce stress levels and anxiety.[121]
4. Researchers have found out in laboratory, animal and human studies that the compounds present in the botanic helps to destroy cancerous cells and protect the body from injury. [122]

Devina H. Collier

5. It protects the brain and central nervous system from different degenerative diseases due to its neuro-protective functions. It helps increase cognitive abilities and is good for increasing the memory in school children. It is also beneficial for improving memory in adults. [123] [124]

6. Rosemary helps in reduction of sensitivity of the body towards different allergens thus decreasing asthma due to its anti-inflammatory properties. [125]

7. In an animal study, Rosemary reduced cellular oxidative stress due to its inhibitory effects on lipid per-oxidation. [126]

8. A recent Rosemary study done on toxic liver cells in humans and rats found that Rosemary has hepatoprotective properties. Rosemary's strong antioxidant properties showed good healing potential against different types of liver injuries. [127] [128]

9. It supports good skin health by protecting it against acne and other fungal, bacterial and viral skin problems. [129]

10. Rosemary is useful as a digestive aid. The botanic helps in decreasing flatulence and

provides a soothing balance to digestive problems. [130]

11. Rosemary is anti-fibrotic. Male Wistar rats with pulmonary fibrosis was treated with the antibiotic Bleomycin, then Rosemary was added before and after treatment with the antibiotic. Scientist found that Rosemary's rosmarinic acids reduced the oxidative stress in lung tissues caused by Bleomycin. Therefore, the lung tissues were less compromised when Rosemary was added to the treatment. Bleomycin is used to treat lung fibrosis.[131]

12. In a recent clinical study, Rosemary leaf extract increased fecal fat excretion in rats. This is good for reducing weight gain. The study concluded that the carnosic content in Rosemary can be effective against metabolic disorders.[132]

13. Rosemary is analgesic. The soothing nature of rosemary oil helps with the reduction of headaches, migraines and inflammation.[133]

14. Radioactive protective. A mice study showed the possibility of Rosemary extract having radioprotective abilities. Swiss albino mice were irradiated with 3 Gy

gamma rays in the presence of 1000 mg/kg body weight of Rosemary extract. White blood cells decreased with radiation, while after 29 days, free radical levels declined (oxidative stress). Amazingly, blood serum levels raised above normal due to Rosemary's potent antioxidant actions against oxidative stress.[134]

15. It shields immunity. Many animal studies have shown that Rosemary has the potential to give immune protection to the body.[135]

16. Rosemary is a mouth freshener. The beautiful and potent scent of this aromatic herb helps in reduction of bad breath and keeps the mouth feeling fresh.[136]

17. It supports Alzheimer's. This deadly old age memory related disease can be improved, and symptoms reduced by Rosemary's neuroprotective properties that lowers oxidative stress in brain cells.[137]

18. In an animal study, Rosemary helped to remove toxins and heal wounds optimally.[138]

~ Great Things ~

He *is* your praise, and He *is* your God, who has done for you these great and awesome things which your eyes have seen. Deuteronomy 10:21

15 Medicinal Purposes of Dill: The Regulator

Dill is one of the most nutritious and healthy herbs. It can be found throughout the world and is used for adding flavor to different dishes. This botanical has natural compounds which have medicinal properties and helps manage many health problems. Scientifically dill is known as Anethum graveolens and the principal medicinal component of the herb, the flavonoids are found in the leaves. Numerous studies have been performed in both animals and humans to give clinical evidence on the effects of dill on health.

Some of the health benefits of this herb are:

1. It helps with sleep regulation. Dill has a calming and relaxing effect on the mind as its minerals help induce proper sleep.[139]
2. Dill is very popular as an anti-gas supporter. It is commonly known for its carminative properties which help in removing the gas out of the digestive track while working to lessen further complications.[140]
3. Dill has high amounts of vitamin A, C, Beta carotene, riboflavin, folic acid and other micro nutrients which help in health protection.[141]
4. It's anti-microbial. This botanic helps to fight against bacterial microorganism thus decreasing and healing infections.[142]
5. In an animal study, Dill has shown digestive aid capabilities. The soothing effect of the herb in addition to the anti-bacterial action helps in digestion and prevents digestive problems like diarrhea and more.[143]
6. Dill is anti-diabetic. It helps to maintain insulin and glucose levels and balance diabetes.[144]
7. The botanic has anti-cancer support properties. It suppresses the proliferation of

tumor cells and fights cancerous growth in the body.[145]

8. The sweet scent of dill helps to maintain fresh breath and the anti-microbial properties helps to act against microorganism causing oral health problems.[146]

9. Due to Dills high content of vitamin C and vitamin A, it has strong antioxidant properties which lessen the formation of free radicals.[147]

10. It is anti-cholesterol. Dill helps to lessen the accumulation of lipids, including cholesterol in the body, thus helping to balance good cardiovascular health.[148]

11. Dill oil has been used to help with reduction of colic symptoms and increase breast milk in mothers that are lactating.[149]

12. The botanic is a natural analgesic and has been found to supports dysmenorrhea pain reduction.[150]

13. Dill is a natural anti-septic due to the eugenol, Vitamin C and anti-microbial properties.[151]

14. Dill has bone protecting properties. It helps to increase calcium in the bone, which

increases the density of bone - especially in osteoporosis.[152]

15. Due is immune protective. The compounds help to increase the overall immunity of the body and thus helps to protect the body from a variety of injurious agents.[153]

~ His Grace is Sufficient ~

And he said unto me, My grace is sufficient for thee: for my strength is made perfect in weakness. Most gladly therefore will I rather glory in my infirmities, that the power of Christ may rest upon me. 2 Corinthians 12:9

15 Medicinal Purposes of Cardamom: The Mediator

Cardamom (Elettaria cardamomum) is an aromatic herb which is used in different cuisine to add flavor to food. The seeds come from the Ginger family. It is also used in different countries throughout South Asia as a medicinal herb for thousands of years. The botanic is extracted from the seeds of the plant Elettaria cardamomum. Thousands of clinical trials have been performed in both animals and human beings to provide evidence of the medicinal benefits of the plant. There are almost no side effects of this herb thus can be taken safely by everyone.

Some of the health benefits of this herb are:

1. It's anti-inflammatory with the ability to decrease free radicals and mediate inflammation and decrease inflammation.[154]
2. Cardamom has a high nutritive value that is anti-microbial and fights detrimental bacteria and fungus. [155]
3. It supports cardiovascular health by helping to protect the heart from chronic diseases, including helping to lower lipid levels and reduce the risk of heart attacks.[156]
4. In an animal study, Cardamom showed anti-depressant properties. It helped reduce mental stress, and anxiety by balancing stress.[157]

5. Cardamom is anti-diabetic. It helps in managing insulin resistance and thus helps in balancing high blood glucose levels in diabetes.[158]

6. Researches have shown that Cardamom helps in lowering blood pressure because it acts as a mild diuretic due to its potassium content. It was also tested against epilepsy in mice and had promising results.[159] [160]

7. This sweet-smelling herb helps to give fresh breath and eliminates microorganisms from the mouth.[161]

8. It has anti-asthmatic properties. Studies have shown that cardamom helps in relieving and decreasing the severity of asthma due to its anti-inflammatory properties.[162]

9. Throat problems: Cardamom is well known for its application for the treatment of throat problems because of its anti-bacterial and anti-inflammatory activities.[163]

10. Cardamom has been found to be anti-carcinogenic by helping to reduce the risk of the growth of tumors at the cellular level. [164]

11. The antibacterial effect of cardamom helps to fight dandruff and help in maintaining proper health of hair.[165]
12. It helps increase blood circulation to skin and supports overall health of skin.[166]
13. Cardamom supports gut bacteria which in turn help gut bacteria boosts gut immunity, and mood.[167]
14. Cardamom is a super antioxidant. The botanic has high amounts of it which act against free radicals and help slow down oxidative stress and acts in premature aging.[168]
15. In an animal study, it helped reduce hiccups because of its antispasmodic activity. It decreases spasm in the diaphragm and that supports hiccups.[169]

~ You Shall Recover ~

And these signs shall follow them that believe; In my name shall they cast out devils; they shall speak with new tongues; They shall take up serpents; and if they drink any deadly thing, it shall not hurt them; they shall lay hands on the sick, and they shall recover. Mark 16:17-18

Devina H. Collier

13 Medicinal Purposes of Ginseng: The Gatekeeper

Ginseng is one of the oldest and the strongest herbs available. It is mainly found in Southeast Asia and Russia. Especially in China, Japan, and Korea. Ginseng belongs to the genus Panax and many herbs from this group are highly beneficial herbs. It is also noteworthy that natural herbs have no major side effects. The roots of this herb are used for medicinal properties. It has been used for hundreds of years as a medicinal herb in ancient civilizations. There are thousands of clinical trials which have been conducted both on animals and humans that provide evidence of the health benefits of the botanic.

1. Ginseng is a highly nutritious herb containing a balance between the micronutrients. It is especially rich in vitamin A, and E.[170]
2. It's anti-diabetic. Researchers have found out that Ginseng helps to control blood glucose levels and thus balance diabetes.[171]
3. Ginseng is a Central Nervous System (CNS) stimulant. The herb acts by making the CNS

active and alert. It helps to enhance memory, concentration and cognitive performance.[172]

4. It supports dandruff. Research has shown that the herb is extremely beneficial for the health of hair and is a potent anti-dandruff agent.[173]

5. Ginseng has the potential to reduce wrinkles and increase the skin quality, thus providing anti-ageing effects.[174]

6. It has been proven to help reduce menstrual pain and discomfort.[175]

7. It supports weight loss by helping to reduce lipid accumulation in the body. It also helps to maintain lipid profile, for example, cholesterol and triglyceride levels.[176]

8. Research has shown that Ginseng is highly effective in supporting erectile dysfunction without any side effects.[177]

9. Research has shown it supports neurodegenerative diseases such as Alzheimer's.[178]

10. Ginseng boosts immunity by protecting immune cells of the body and supports inflammation.[179]

11. A special type of Ginseng, the Korean Red Ginseng acts against virus to help eliminate it out of the body.[180]
12. Ginseng is a strong antioxidant and thus is able to reduce the risk of cancer cells formation and growth.[181]
13. It is helpful against cardiovascular problems, such as heart attack, thus a good support for major cardiovascular diseases.[182]

~ Worthy to be Praised ~

Saying with a loud voice, Worthy is the Lamb that was slain to receive power, and riches, and wisdom, and strength, and honour, and glory, and blessing. Revelation 5:12

Devina H. Collier

Evidence-Based Herbal References

HOLY BASIL

[1] P. H. Amvam Zollo. L. Biyiti. F. Tchoumbougnang. C. Menut. G. Lamaty. Ph. Bouchet. Aromatic plants of Tropical Central Africa. Part XXXII. Chemical composition and antifungal activity of thirteen essential oils from aromatic plants of Cameroon. Flavour and Fragrance Journal.

[2] S.C. Umerie. H.U. Anaso. L.J.C. Anyasoro. Insecticidal potentials of Ocimum basilicum leaf-extract. Bioresource Technology. Volume 64, Issue 3, June 1998, Pages 237-239.

[3] Marta Ferreira Maia, Sarah J Moore. Plant-based insect repellents: a review of their efficacy, development and testing. 2011 Mar 15. Bio Med Central Malaria Journal.

[4] Cabdirect.org. CAB Abstracts and Global Health

[5] C. Leigh Broadhurst. Marilyn M. Polansky. Richard A. Anderson. Insulin-like Biological Activity of Culinary and Medicinal Plant Aqueous Extracts in Vitro. Journal of Agricultural and Food Chemistry. 2000, 48 (3), pp 849–852

[6] Pooja Agarwal, L Nagesh, Murlikrishnan. Evaluation of the antimicrobial activity of various concentrations of Tulsi (Ocimum sanctum) extract against Streptococcus mutans: An in vitro study. Indian Journal of Dental Research. 2010. Volume: 21. Issue: 3. Page: 357-359

[7] Chiang LC1. Ng LT. Cheng PW. Chiang W. Lin CC. Antiviral activities of extracts and selected pure constituents of Ocimum basilicum. Clinical and Experimental Pharmacology and Physiology. 2005 Oct;32(10):811-6.

[8] Lianet Monzote. Oswald Alarcón. William N. Setzer. Antiprotozoal Activity of Essential Oils: Review Article. Agriculturae Conspectus Scientifi cus . Vol. 77 (2012) No. 4 (167-175).

[9] P. Misra. N. L. Pal. P. Y. Guru. J. C. Katiyar. J. S. Tandon. International Journal of Pharmacognosy. Antimalarial Activity of Traditional Plants against Erythrocytic Stages of Plasmodium berghei.

[10] Kanojiya D1. Shanker D1. Sudan V2. Jaiswal AK1. Parashar R. Anthelmintic activity of Ocimum sanctum leaf

extract against ovine gastrointestinal nematodes in India. Research in Veterinary Science. 2015 Apr;99:165-70.

[11] J Javanmardi. C Stushnoff. E Locke. J.M. Vivanco. Antioxidant activity and total phenolic content of Iranian Ocimum accessions. Food Chemistry. Volume 83, Issue 4, December 2003, Pages 547-550.

[12] Negar Jamshidi. Marc M. Cohen. The Clinical Efficacy and Safety of Tulsi in Humans: A Systematic Review of the Literature. Evidence-Based Complementary and Alternative Medicine. 2017.

[13] Shadi Sarahroodi. Somayyeh Esmaeili. Peyman Mikaili. Zahra Hemmati. Yousof Saberi. The effects of green Ocimum basilicum hydroalcoholic extract on retention and retrieval of memory in mice. Ancient Science of Life. 2012 Apr-Jun; 31(4): 185–189.

[14] Jyoti S. Satendra S. Sushma S. Anjana T. Shashi S. Antistressor activity of Ocimum sanctum (Tulsi) against experimentally induced oxidative stress in rabbits. Methods and Findings in Experimental and Clinical Pharmacology. 2007 Jul-Aug;29(6):411-6.

[15] Surender Singh, D K Majumdar. Effect of Fixed Oil of Ocimum sanctum against Experimentally Induced Arthritis and Joint Edema in Laboratory Animals. International Journal of Pharmacognosy. Sep 29 2008. Pages 218-222.

[16] Ilhan Kaya. Nazife Yigit. Mehlika Benli. Antimicrobial Activity of Various Extracts of Ocimum Basilicum L. and Observation of the Inhibition Effect on Bacterial Cells by Use of Scanning Electron Microscopy. African Journal of Traditional, Complementary and Alternative medicines. 2008; 5(4): 363–369.

[17] P Uma Devi. Radioprotective, anticarcinogenic and antioxidant properties of the Indian holy basil, Ocimum sanctum (Tulasi). Review Article. Indian Journal of Experimental Biology Vol. 39, March 2001, pp. 185-190

[18] A Review on Herbal Therapy for Respiratory Ailments. International Journal of Life Science & Pharma Research. Review Article ISSN 2250-0480 VOL 6/ ISSUE 2/APRIL 2016

[19] Marc Maurice Cohen. Tulsi - Ocimum sanctum: A herb for all reasons. Journal of Ayurveda and Integrative Medicine. 2014 Oct-Dec; 5(4): 251–259.

[20] Shankar Mondal. Saurabh Varma. Vishwa Deepak Bamola.

Satya Narayan Naik. Bijay Ranjan Mirdha. Madan Mohan Padhi. Nalin Mehta. Sushil Chandra Mahapatra. Double-blinded randomized controlled trial for immunomodulatory effects of Tulsi (Ocimum sanctum Linn.) leaf extract on healthy volunteers. Journal of Ethnopharmacology. Volume 136, Issue 3, 14 July 2011, Pages 452-456.

[21] Surender Singha. D.K. Majumdara. H.M.S. Rehan. Evaluation of anti-inflammatory potential of fixed oil of Ocimum sanctum (Holybasil) and its possible mechanism of action. Journal of Ethnopharmacology. Volume 54, Issue 1, October 1996, Pages 19-26.

[22] Umashanker et al. Srivastava Shruti. International Journal of Research in Pharmacy and Chemistry. Review Article. IJRPC 2011, 1(4) ISSN: 2231-2781

[23] Brian Krans. Ana Gotter. The Health Benefits of Holy Basil. Healthline 2017. Media

[24] Kingshuk Lahon. Swarnamoni Das. Hepatoprotective activity of Ocimum sanctum alcoholic leaf extract against paracetamol-induced liver damage in Albino rats. 2011 Jan-Mar; 3(1): 13–18.

[25] Marc Maurice Cohen. Tulsi - Ocimum sanctum: A herb for all reasons. Journal of Ayurveda and Integrative Medicine. 2014 Oct-Dec; 5(4): 251–259.

GARLIC

[26] Morihara N. Nishihama T. Ushijima M. Ide N. Takeda H. Hayama M. Garlic as an anti-fatigue agent. Molecular Nutrition & Food Research. 2007 Nov;51(11):1329-34.

[27] Self NutritionData. Know what you eat.

[28] Borek C. Antioxidant health effects of aged garlic extract. Journal of Nutrition. 2001 March.

[29] Josling P. Preventing the common cold with a garlic supplement: A double-blind, placebo-controlled survey. Advances in Therapy - Journals. 2001 Jul-Aug;18(4):189-93.

[30] Iram Gull. Mariam Saeed. Halima Shaukat. Shahbaz M Aslam. Zahoor Qadir Samra. Amin M Athar. Inhibitory effect of Allium sativum and Zingiber officinale extracts on clinically important drug resistant pathogenic bacteria. Annals of Clinical Microbiology and Antimicrobials. 201211:8

[31] Young-Min Lee. Oh-Cheon Gweon. Yeong-Ju Seo. Jieun Im.

Min-Jung Kang. Myo-Jeong Kim. Jung-In Kim. Antioxidant effect of garlic and aged black garlic in animal model of type 2 diabetes mellitus. Nutrition Research and Practice. 2009 Summer; 3(2): 156–161.

[32] Danan Wang. Yonghui Feng. Jun Liu. Jianzhong Yan. Meiru Wang. Jin-ichi Sasaki. Changlong Lu. Black Garlic (Allium sativum) Extracts Enhance the Immune System. Medicinal and Aromatic Plant Science and Biotechnology. Global Science Books.

[33] Knowles LM. Milner JA. Diallyl disulfide induces ERK phosphorylation and alters gene expression profiles in human colon tumor cells. Journal of Nutrition. 2003 Sep;133(9):2901-6.

[34] Kianoush S. Balali-Mood M. Mousavi SR. Moradi V. Sadeghi M. Dadpour B. Rajabi O. Shakeri MT. Comparison of therapeutic effects of garlic and d-Penicillamine in patients with chronic occupational lead poisoning. Basic & Clinical Pharmacology & Toxicology. 2012 May.

[35] Williams FM. Skinner J. Spector TD. Cassidy A. Clark IM. Davidson RM. MacGregor AJ. Dietary garlic and hip osteoarthritis: evidence of a protective effect and putative mechanism of action. 2010 Dec 8.

[36] Reinhart KM, Talati R, White CM, Coleman CI. The impact of garlic on lipid parameters: a systematic review and meta-analysis. Nutrition Research Reviews: Journals. 2009 Jun;22(1):39-48

[37] Kim MJ. Kim HK. Effect of garlic on high fat induced obesity. Acta Biologica Hungarica. 2011 September.

[38] Sial AY. Ahmad SI. Study of the hypotensive action of garlic extract in experimental animals. Journal of the Pakistan Medical Association. 1982 October.

[39] Adedayo O Ademiluyi. Ganiyu Oboh. Tosin R Owoloye. Oluwaseun J Agbebi. Modulatory effects of dietary inclusion of garlic (Allium sativum) on gentamycin-induced hepatotoxicity and oxidative stress in rats. Asian Pacific Journal of Tropical Biomedicine. 2013 Jun; 3(6): 470–475.

[40] Yousuf S. Ahmad A. Khan A. Manzoor N. Khan LA. Effect of garlic-derived allyl sulphides on morphogenesis and hydrolytic enzyme secretion in Candida albicans. Medical Mycology Journal. 2011 May;49(4):444-8.

[41] Guo NL. Lu DP. Woods GL. Reed E. Zhou GZ. Zhang LB. Waldman RH. Demonstration of the anti-viral activity of

garlic extract against human cytomegalovirus in vitro. Chinese Medical Journal. 993 Feb;106(2):93-6.

42 Jain RC. Effect of garlic on serum lipids, coagulability and fibrinolytic activity of blood. The American Journal of Clinical Nutrition. 1977 Sep;30(9):1380-1.

43 Leyla Bayan. Peir Hossain Koulivand. Ali Gorji. Garlic: A review of potential therapeutic effects. Avicenna Journal of Phytomedicine. 2014 Jan-Feb; 4(1): 1–14.

GINGER

44 Ponmurugan Karuppiah. Shyamkumar Rajaram. Antibacterial effect of Allium sativum cloves and Zingiber officinale rhizomes against multiple-drug resistant clinical pathogens. Asian Pacific Journal of Tropical Biomedicine. 2012 Aug; 2(8): 597–601.

45 Pseudomonas Infection. WebMD.com

46 Youngsoo Kim. British Journal of Pharmacology 2012 Sep; 167(1): 128–140.

47 Kalra M. Khatak M. Khatak S. International Journal of Drug Development & Research. Jan-March 2011. Vol. 3. Issue 1. ISSN 0975-9344.

48 Patrick B. Wilson. Ginger (Zingiber officinale) as an Analgesic and Ergogenic Aid in Sport: A Systemic Review. Journal of Strength & Conditioning Research: October 2015 - Volume 29 - Issue 10 - p 2980–2995.

49 Young-Ho Jin. Korean Journal Physiol Pharmacol. 2014 Apr;18(2):149-153.

50 Thomson M. Corbin R. Leung L. Effects of ginger for nausea and vomiting in early pregnancy: a meta-analysis. Journal of the American Board of Family Medicine.

51 Kengliang Wu. Effects of ginger on gastric emptying and motility in healthy humans. European Journal of Gastroenterology & Hepatology. 2008 May;20(5):436-40.

52 Kim Yu. Toxicology and Applied Pharmacology6-Shogaol, an active compound of ginger, alleviates allergic dermatitis-like skin lesions via cytokine inhibition by activating the Nrf2 pathway. 2016 November.

53 Ghayur MN. Ginger attenuates acetylcholine-induced contraction and Ca2+ signalling in murine airway smooth muscle cells. Canadian Journal of Physiology and Pharmacology.

54 Mahmoud YI. Ginger and alpha lipoic acid ameliorate age-

related ultrastructural changes in rat liver. Biotechnic & Histochemistry 2016;91(2):86-95.
55 Kazumi Yagasaki. Inhibitory effect of gingerol on the proliferation and invasion of hepatoma cells in culture. Cytotechnology. 2008 Jun; 57(2): 129–136.
56 Hashim S. Modulatory effects of essential oils from spices on the formation of DNA adduct by aflatoxin B1 in vitro. Nutrition and Cancer. 1994;21(2):169-75.
57 Ghayur MN. Ginger lowers blood pressure through blockade of voltage-dependent calcium channels. Journal of Cardiovascular Pharmacology. 2005 Jan;45(1):74-80.
58 Hong-Kai Gao. The effect of ginger supplementation on serum C-reactive protein, lipid profile and glycaemia: a systematic review and meta-analysis. Food & Nutrition Research. 2016; 60: 10.3402/fnr.v60.32613.
59 Rasha Asu. Comparative evaluation of the efficacy of ginger and orlistat on obesity management, pancreatic lipase and liver peroxisomal catalase enzyme in male albino rats. European Review for Medical and Pharmacological Sciences
60 Farzad Shidfar. The Effects of Ginger on Fasting Blood Sugar, Hemoglobin A1c, Apolipoprotein B, Apolipoprotein A-I and Malondialdehyde in Type 2 Diabetic Patients. Iranian Journal of Pharmaceutical Research. 2015 Winter; 14(1): 131–140.
61 Rahimlou M. Yari Z. Hekmatdoost A. Alavian SM. Keshavarz SA. Ginger Supplementation in Nonalcoholic Fatty Liver Disease: A Randomized, Double-Blind, Placebo-Controlled Pilot Study. Hepatitis Monthly - Journals. 2016 Jan 23;16(1):e34897.
62 Mohammad Sharrif Moghaddasi. Hamed Haddad Kashani. Ginger (Zingiber officinale): A review. Journal of Medicinal Plants Research Vol. 6(26), pp. 4255-4258,11 July, 2012
63 Jung San Chang. Kuo Chih Wang. Chia Feng Ye. Den En Shieh. Lien Chai Chiang. Fresh ginger (Zingiber officinale) has anti-viral activity against human respiratory syncytial virus in human respiratory tract cell lines. Journal of Ethnopharmacology. Volume 145, Issue 1, 9 January 2013, Pages 146-151.
64 Ahmed Moussa. Djebli Noureddine. Hammoudi SM. Aissat Saad. Akila Bourabeh. Hemida Houari. Additive potential of ginger starch on antifungal potency of honey against

Candida albicans. Asian Pacific Journal of Tropical Biomedicine. 2012 Apr; 2(4): 253–255.

CINNAMON

[65] Bolin Qin, M.D., Ph.D., Kiran S. Panickar. Richard A. Anderson, Ph.D., C.N.S. Cinnamon: Potential Role in the Prevention of Insulin Resistance, Metabolic Syndrome, and Type 2 Diabetes. Journal of Diabetes Science and Technology. 2010 May; 4(3): 685–693.

[66] Azam Borzoeia. Maryam Rafraf Shirin Niromanesh. Laya Farzadi. Fateme Narimanie. Farideh Doostan. Effects of cinnamon supplementation on antioxidant status and serum lipids in women with polycystic ovary syndrome. Journal of Traditional and Complementary Medicine. January 2017.

[67] Khan A, Safdar M. Ali Khan MM. Khattak KN. Anderson RA. Cinnamon improves glucose and lipids of people with type 2 diabetes. Diabetes Care. 2003 Dec;26(12):3215-8.

[68] Hamid Mollazadeh. Hossein Hosseinzadeh. Cinnamon effects on metabolic syndrome: a review based on its mechanisms. Iranian Journal of Basic Medical Sciences. 2016 Dec; 19(12): 1258–1270.

[69] Joung-Woo Hong. Ga-Eun Yang. Yoon Bum Kim. Seok Hyun Eom. Jae-Hwan Lew. Hee Kang. Anti-inflammatory activity of cinnamon water extract in vivo and in vitro LPS-induced models. BMC Complementary and Alternative Medicine. July 2012.

[70] Seyed Fazel Nabavi. Arianna Di Lorenzo. Morteza Izadi. Eduardo Sobarzo-Sánchez. Maria Daglia. Seyed Mohammad Nabavi. Antibacterial Effects of Cinnamon: From Farm to Food, Cosmetic and Pharmaceutical Industries. Nutrients. 2015 Sep; 7(9): 7729–7748.

[71] Pasupuleti Visweswara Rao. Siew Hua Gan. Cinnamon: A Multifaceted Medicinal Plant. Evidence-Based Complementary and Alternative Medicine. 2014; 2014: 642942.

[72] Yan Shen. Liu-Nan Jia. Natsumi Honma. Takashi Hosono. Toyohiko Ariga. Taiichiro Seki. Beneficial Effects of Cinnamon on the Metabolic Syndrome, Inflammation, and Pain, and Mechanisms Underlying These Effects – A Review. Journal of Traditional and Complementary Medicine. 2012 Jan-Mar; 2(1): 27–32.

73 Molouk Jaafarpour. Masoud Hatefi. Fatemeh Najafi. Javaher Khajavikhan. Ali Khani. The Effect of Cinnamon on Menstrual Bleeding and Systemic Symptoms With Primary Dysmenorrhea. Iranian Red Crescent Medical Journal. 2015 Apr; 17(4): e27032.

74 Daniel H. Kort, MD, Roger A. Lobo, MD. Preliminary evidence that cinnamon improves menstrual cyclicity in women with polycystic ovary syndrome: a randomized controlled trial. American Journal of Obstetrics & Gynecology. November 2014 Volume 211, Issue 5, Pages 487.e1–487.e6

75 Singh HB. Srivastava M. Singh AB. Srivastava AK. Cinnamon bark oil, a potent fungitoxicant against fungi causing respiratory tract mycoses. Centre for Biochemical Technology, Delhi, India. Allergy. 1995 Dec;50(12):995-9.

76 B. Raudenbush. T. Sears. R. Grayhem. I. Wilson.. Effects of peppermint and cinnamon odor administration on simulated driving alertness, mood and workload. Researchgate.net.

77 Rafie Hamidpour. Mohsen Hamidpour. Soheila Hamidpour. Mina Shahlari. Cinnamon from the selection of traditional applications to its novel effects on the inhibition of angiogenesis in cancer cells and prevention of Alzheimer's disease, and a series of functions such as antioxidant, anticholesterol, antidiabetes, antibacterial, antifungal, nematicidal, acaracidal, and repellent activities. Journal of Traditional and Complementary Medicine. 2015 Apr; 5(2): 66–70.

78 Pasupuleti Visweswara Rao. Siew Hua Gan. Cinnamon: A Multifaceted Medicinal Plant. Evidence-Based Complementary and Alternative Medicine. 2014; 2014: 642942.

79 Abhinav Singh. Bharathi Purohit. Tooth brushing, oil pulling and tissue regeneration: A review of holistic approaches to oral health. Journal of Ayurveda and Integrative Medicine. 2011 Apr-Jun; 2(2): 64–68.

80 Akilen R. Tsiami A. Devendra D. Robinson N. Glycated haemoglobin and blood pressure-lowering effect of cinnamon in multi-ethnic Type 2 diabetic patients in the UK: A randomized, placebo-controlled, double-blind clinical trial. Diabetic Medicine. 2010 Oct;27(10):1159-67.

81 Gupta C. Kumari A. Garg AP. Catanzaro R. Marotta F.

Comparative study of cinnamon oil and clove oil on some oral microbiota. Acta Bio-Medica. 2011 Dec;82(3):197-9.

[82] Takasao N. Tsuji-Naito K. Ishikura S. Tamura A. Akagawa M. Cinnamon extract promotes type I collagen biosynthesis via activation of IGF-I signaling in human dermal fibroblasts. Journal of Agricultural and Food Chemistry. 2012 Feb 8;60(5):1193-200.

[83] Said S. Moselhy. Husein K. H. Ali. Hepatoprotective effect of Cinnamon extracts against carbon tetrachloride induced oxidative stress and liver injury in rats. Biological Research. 42: 93-98,2009.

LAVENDER

[84] Sasannejad P. Saeedi M.a. Shoeibi A. Gorji A. Abbasi M. Foroughipour M. Lavender Essential Oil in the Treatment of Migraine Headache: A Placebo-Controlled Clinical Trial. European Neurology. 2012;67:288–291.

[85] Shu-Lan Chen RN, MSN. Chung-Hey Chen RN, PhD. Effects of Lavender Tea on Fatigue, Depression, and Maternal-Infant Attachment in Sleep-Disturbed Postnatal Women. Worldviews on Evidence-Based Nursing. Volume 12, Issue 6.

[86] Elisa Boody. Lavender as a Sleep Aid. Health Psychology. Vanderbilt University. October 5, 2009.

[87] Peir Hossein Koulivand. Maryam Khaleghi Ghadiri. Ali Gorji. Lavender and the Nervous System. Evidence-Based Complementary and Alternative Medicine. 2013; 2013: 681304.

[88] Nilima Thosar. Silpi Basak. Rakesh N. Bahadure. Monali Rajurkar. Antimicrobial efficacy of five essential oils against oral pathogens: An in vitro study. European Journal of Dentistry. 2013 Sep; 7(Suppl 1): S71–S77.

[89] C. Blamey. Case History of Infected Eczema Treated with Essential Oils. Grand Rounds Journal. Speciality: Alternative TherapiesVol 1 pages 11–14.

[90] Jason A. Hawrelak, PhD,, BNat(Hons). Trudi Cattley, BSci. Stephen P. Myers, PhD, BMed, ND. Essential Oils in the Treatment of Intestinal Dysbiosis: A Preliminary In vitro Study. Alternative Medicine Review Volume 14, Number 4 2009.

[91] Zu Y. Yu H. Liang L, Fu Y. Efferth T. Liu X. Wu N. Activities of ten essential oils towards Propionibacterium acnes and

PC-3, A-549 and MCF-7 cancer cells. Molecules. 2010 Apr 30;15(5):3200-10.
92 Sienkiewicz M. Łysakowska M. Ciećwierz J. Denys P. Kowalczyk E. Antibacterial activity of thyme and lavender essential oils. Medicinal Chemistry. 2011 Nov;7(6):674-89.
93 Hiroko-Miyuki Mori. Hiroshi Kawanami. Hirohisa Kawahata. Motokuni Aoki. Wound healing potential of lavender oil by acceleration of granulation and wound contraction through induction of TGF-β in a rat model. BMC Complementary and Alternative Medicine. 2016; 16: 144.
94 Jane Buckle, PhD, MA, RN. Aromatherapy and Diabetes. Diabetes Spectrum 2001 Aug; 14(3): 124-126.
95 R Nikjou. R Kazemzadeh. M Rostamnegad. S Moshfegi. M Karimollahi. H Salehi. The Effect of Lavender Aromatherapy on the Pain Severity of Primary Dysmenorrhea: A Triple-blind Randomized Clinical Trial. Annals of Medical and Health Sciences Research. 2016 Jul-Aug; 6(4): 211–215.
96 Health Benefits of Lavender Essential Oil. TheResearchpedia.com
97 Aromatherapy. Cancer Research UK. Cancerresearchuk.org
98 Boo Hyeong Lee. Jae Soon Lee. Young Chul Kim. Hair Growth-Promoting Effects of Lavender Oil in C57BL/6 Mice. Toxicology Research. 2016 Apr; 32(2): 103–108.
99 Shiina Y. Funabashi N. Lee K. Toyoda T. Sekine T. Honjo S. Hasegawa R. Kawata T. Wakatsuki Y. Hayashi S. Murakami S, Koike K. Daimon M. Komuro I. Relaxation effects of lavender aromatherapy improve coronary flow velocity reserve in healthy men evaluated by transthoracic Doppler echocardiography. International Journal of Cardiology. 2008 Sep 26;129(2):193-7. Epub 2007 Aug 8.
100 Cavanagh HM. Wilkinson JM. Biological activities of lavender essential oil. Phytotherapy Research. 2002 Jun;16(4):301-8.
101 Peir Hossein Koulivand. Maryam Khaleghi Ghadiri. Ali Gorji. Lavender and the Nervous System. Evidence-Based Complementary and Alternative Medicine. Volume 2013 (2013), Article ID 681304, 10 pages.

CAYENNE PEPPER
102 Keith Jones, PhD, UC's department of pharmacology and

cell biophysics. Study Shows Common Pain Cream Could Protect Heart During Attack. University of Cincinnati. Academic Health Center Public Relations & Communications.

[103] K D K Ahuja. I K Robertson. D P Geraghty. M J Ball. The effect of 4-week chilli supplementation on metabolic and arterial function in humans. European Journal of Clinical Nutrition 61, 326–333. 2007.

[104] Clegg ME. Golsorkhi M. Henry CJ. Combined medium-chain triglyceride and chilli feeding increases diet-induced thermogenesis in normal-weight humans. European Journal of Nutrition. 2013 Sep;52(6):1579-85.

[105] Janssens PL. Hursel R. Martens EA. Westerterp-Plantenga MS. Acute effects of capsaicin on energy expenditure and fat oxidation in negative energy balance. Public Library of Science. 2013 Jul 2;8(7):e67786.

[106] J. B. Van Rijswijk. E. L. Boeke. J. M. Keizer. P. G. H. Mulder. H. M. Blom. W. J. Fokkens. Intranasal capsaicin reduces nasal hyperreactivity in idiopathic rhinitis: a double-blind randomized application regimen study. European Journal of Allergy & Clinical Immunology. 10 July 2003

[107] Bernstein JE. Parish LC. Rapaport M. Rosenbaum MM,. Roenigk HH Jr. Effects of topically applied capsaicin on moderate and severe psoriasis vulgaris. Journal of the American Academy of Dermatology. 1986 Sep;15(3):504-7.

[108] Kiran DK Ahuja. Iain K Robertson. Dominic P Geraghty. Madeleine J Ball. Effects of chili consumption on postprandial glucose, insulin, and energy metabolism. American Society for Clinical Nutrition. 2006.

[109] Dachun Yang. Zhidan Luo. Shuangtao Ma. Wing Tak Wong. Liqun Ma. Jian Zhong. Hongbo He. Zhigang Zhao. Tingbing Cao. Zhencheng Yan. Daoyan Liu. Daoyan Liu. William J. Arendshorst. Yu Huang. Martin Tepel. Zhiming Zhu. Activation of TRPV1 by Dietary Capsaicin Improves Endothelium-Dependent Vasorelaxation and Prevents Hypertension. Cell Metabolism Journal. Volume 12, Issue 2, p130–141, 4 August 2010

[110] Capsaicin may have important potential for promoting vascular and metabolic health. Mark F McCarty. James J DiNicolantonio. James H O'Keefe. BMJ. Cardiac risk factors

and prevention. Volume 2, Issue 1.
[111] Hussain MS. Chandrasekhara N. Biliary proteins from hepatic bile of rats fed curcumin or capsaicin inhibit cholesterol crystal nucleation in supersaturated model bile. Indian Journal of Biochemistry & Biophysics 01 Oct 1994, 31(5):407-412.
[112] Sicuteri, Federigo; Fusco, Bruno M.; Marabini, Simone; Campagnolo, Valter; Maggi, Carlo Alberto; Geppetti, Pierangelo; Fanciullacci, Marcello. Beneficial Effect of Capsaicin Application to the Nasal Mucosa in Cluster Headache. Clinical Journal of Pain: March 1989.
[113] Maji AK, Banerji P. Phytochemistry and gastrointestinal benefits of the medicinal spice, Capsicum annuum L. (Chilli): a review. Journal of Complementary & Integrative Medicine. 2016 Jun 1;13(2):97-122.
[114] Hunter Groninger, M.D. Randall E. Schisler, M.D. Topical Capsaicin for Neuropathic Pain #255. Journal of Palliative Medicine. 2012 Aug; 15(8): 946–947.
[115] MedlinePlus Trusted Health Information for You. Herbs and Supplements → Capsicum.
[116] Surh YJ. More than spice: capsaicin in hot chili peppers makes tumor cells commit suicide. Hail N Jr. Lotan R. Examining the role of mitochondrial respiration in vanilloid-induced apoptosis. The Journal of the National Cancer Institute. 2002 Sep 4;94(17):1263-5. 1281-92
[117] Surh YJ. Journal of the National Cancer Institute, Volume 94, Issue 17, 4 September 2002, Pages 1263–1265
[118] Rosa A. Deiana M. Casu V. Paccagnini S. Appendino G, Ballero M. Dessí MA. Antioxidant activity of capsinoids. Journal of Agricultural and Food Chemistry. 2002 Dec 4;50(25):7396-401.

ROSEMARY
[119] Naemura A. Ura M. Yamashita T. Arai R. Yamamoto J. Long-term intake of rosemary and common thyme herbs inhibits experimental thrombosis without prolongation of bleeding time. Thrombosis Research - Journal. 2008;122(4):517-22
[120] Moyosoluwa Oluwatuyi. Glenn W. Kaatz. Simon Gibbons. Antibacterial and resistance modifying activity of Rosmarinus officinalis. Phytochemistry. Volume 65, Issue 24, Pages 3175-3292. Dec 2004.

[121] McCaffrey R. Thomas DJ. Kinzelman AO. The effects of lavender and rosemary essential oils on test-taking anxiety among graduate nursing students. Holistic Nursing Practice - Journals. 2009 Mar-Apr;23(2):88-93

[122] Jessy Moore, Michael Yousef, Evangelia Tsiani. Anticancer Effects of Rosemary (Rosmarinus officinalis L.) Extract and Rosemary Extract Polyphenols. Nutrients. 2016 Nov; 8(11): 731.

[123] Rosmarinus officinalis. Complementary and Alternative Medicine Guide. University of Maryland Medical Center.

[124] Mark Moss. Lorraine Oliver. Plasma 1,8-cineole correlates with cognitive performance following exposure to rosemary essential oil aroma. Therapeutic Advances in Psychopharmacology - Journals. 2012 Jun; 2(3): 103–113.

[125] Winai Sayorwan. Nijsiri Ruangrungsi. Teerut Piriyapunyporn. Tapanee Hongratanaworakit. Naiphinich Kotchabhakdi. Vorasith Siripornpanich. Effects of Inhaled Rosemary Oil on Subjective Feelings and Activities of the Nervous System. Scientia Pharmaceutica. 2013 Apr-Jun; 81(2): 531–542.

[126] I. Takaki, L.E. Bersani-Amado, A. Vendruscolo, S.M. Sartoretto, S.P. Diniz, C.A. Bersani-Amado, and R.K.N. Cuman. Anti-Inflammatory and Antinociceptive Effects of Rosmarinus officinalis L. Essential Oil in Experimental Animal Models. Journal of Medicinal Food. December 2008, 11(4): 741-746

[127] J.I Sotelo-Félixa. D Martinez-Fong. P Muriel. R.L Santill. Castillo. P Yahuaca. Evaluation of the effectiveness of Rosmarinus officinalis (Lamiaceae) in the alleviation of carbon tetrachloride-induced acute hepatotoxicity in the rat. Journal of Ethnopharmacology. Volume 81, Issue 2, July 2002, Pages 145-154.

[128] Aleksandar Rašković. Isidora Milanović. Nebojša Pavlović. Tatjana Ćebović. Saša Vukmirović. Momir Mikov. Antioxidant activity of rosemary (Rosmarinus officinalis L.) essential oil and its hepatoprotective potential. BMC Complementary and Alternative Medicine. 2014; 14: 225.

[129] Ramachandran C. Quirin KW. Escalon E. Melnick SJ. Improved neuroprotective effects by combining Bacopa monnieri and Rosmarinus officinalis supercritical CO2 extracts.Journal of Evidence-Based Complementary & Alternative Medicine. 2014 Apr;19(2):119-27

Devina H. Collier

130 Rosemary is an herb. Oil is extracted from the leaf and used to make medicine. Natural Medicines Comprehensive Database. Webmd.com

131 Sana Bahri. Ridha Ben Ali. Khaoula Gasmi. Mona Mlika. Saloua Fazaa. Riadh Ksouri. Raja Serairi. Saloua Jameleddine. Vadim Shlyonsky. Prophylactic and curative effect of rosemary leaves extract in a bleomycin model of pulmonary fibrosis. Journal Pharmaceutical Biology Volume 55, 2017 - Issue 1

132 Alvin Ibarra. Julien Cases. Marc Roller. Amparo Chiralt-Boix. Aure´lie Coussaert. Christophe Ripoll.. British Journal of Nutrition (2011), page 1 of 8. Carnosic acid-rich rosemary (Rosmarinus officinalis L.) leaf extract limits.

133 Medically reviewed by Debra Rose Wilson, PhD, MSN, RN, IBCLC, AHN-BC, CHT on April 26, 2017 — Written by Ana Gotter 5 Essential Oils for Headaches and Migraines. Healthline.com

134 G Sancheti, PK Goyal. Prevention Of Radiation Induced Hematological Alterations By Medicinal Plant Rosmarinus officinalis, In Mice. African Journal of Traditional, Complementary and Alternative Medicines. Vol 4, No 2. 2007

135 Babu US. Wiesenfeld PL. Jenkins MY. Effect of dietary rosemary extract on cell-mediated immunity of young rats. Plant Foods Human Nutrition. 1999;53(2):169-74.

136 Solomon Habtemariam. The Therapeutic Potential of Rosemary (Rosmarinus officinalis) Diterpenes for Alzheimer's Disease. Evidence Based Complement Alternative Medicine. Jan 28, 2016

137 Kennedy. David O. Scholey. Andrew B. The Psychopharmacology of European Herbs with Cognition-Enhancing Properties. Pharmaceutical Design, Volume 12, Number 35.

138 Healing potential of Rosmarinus officinalis L. on full-thickness excision cutaneous wounds in alloxan-induced-diabetic BALB/c mice. Journal of Ethnopharmacology. Volume 131, Issue 2, 15 September 2010, Pages 443-450

DILL
139 Jerome Sarris. Alexander Panossian. Isaac Schweitzer. Con Stough. Andrew Scholey. Herbal medicine for depression, anxiety and insomnia: A review of psychopharmacology

and clinical evidence. European Neuropsychopharmacology. Volume 21, Issue 12, December 2011, Pages 841-860.

[140] Nasrin Fazel. Akbar Pejhan. Mohsen Taghizadeh. Yaser Tabarraei. Nasrin Sharifi. Effects of Anethum graveolens L. (Dill) essential oil on the intensity of retained intestinal gas, flatulence and pain after cesarean section: A randomized, double-blind placebo-controlled trial. Journal of Herbal Medicine. Volume 8, June 2017, Pages 8-13.

[141] Jacek Słupski. Zofia Lisiewska. Waldemar Kmiecik. Contents of macro and microelements in fresh and frozen dill (Anethum graveolens L.). Food Chemistry. Volume 91, Issue 4, August 2005, Pages 737-743.

[142] Mallappa Kumara Swamy. Mohd Sayeed Akhtar. Uma Rani Sinniah. Antimicrobial Properties of Plant Essential Oils against Human Pathogens and Their Mode of Action: An Updated Review. Evidence Based Complement Alternative Medicine. Dec 20, 2016.

[143] Mohsen Naseri. Faraz Mojab. Mahmood Khodadoost. Mohammad Kamalinejad. Ali Davati. Rasol Choopani. Abbas Hasheminejad. Zahra Bararpoor. Shamsa Shariatpanahi. Majid Emtiazy. The Study of Anti-Inflammatory Activity of Oil-Based Dill (Anethum graveolens L.) Extract Used Topically in Formalin-Induced Inflammation Male Rat Paw. Iranian Journal of Pharmaceutical Research. 2012 Autumn; 11(4): 1169–1174

[144] Mohammad Taghi Goodarzi. Iraj Khodadadi. Heidar Tavilani. Ebrahim Abbasi Oshaghi. The Role of Anethum graveolens L. (Dill) in the Management of Diabetes. Journal Tropical Medicine. Oct 18, 2016.

[145] Victor V. Semenov. Dmitry V. Tsyganov. Marina N. Semenova. Roman N. Chuprov-Netochin. Mikhail M. Raihstat. Leonid D. Konyushkin. Polina B. Volynchuk. Elena I. Victor V. Semenov. Dmitry V. Tsyganov. Marina N. Semenova. Roman N. Chuprov-Netochin. Mikhail M. Raihstat. Leonid D. Konyushkin. Polina B. Volynchuk. Elena I. Marusich. Vera V. Nazarenko. Sergey V. Leonov. Alex S. Kiselyov. Journal of Natural Products. Moscow Institute of Physics and Technology. April 21, 2016.

[146] Shruthi Eshwar. Rekha K. Vipin Jain. Supriya Manvi. Shivani Kohli. Shekhar Bhatia. Comparison of Dill Seed Oil

Mouth Rinse and Chlorhexidine Mouth Rinse on Plaque
Levels and Gingivitis - A Double Blind Randomized Clinical
Trial. The Open Dentistry Journal. May 2016. 10: 207–213

147 Ebrahim Abbasi Oshaghi. PhD. Iraj Khodadadi, PhD. Heidar
Tavilani, PhD. Mohammad Taghi Goodarzi, PhD. Aqueous
Extract of Anethum Graveolens L. has Potential Antioxidant
and Antiglycation Effects.

148 Masoume Mansouri. Neda Nayebi. Abasali keshtkar. Shirin
Hasani-Ranjbar. Eghbal Taheri. Bagher Larijani. The effect
of 12 weeks Anethum graveolens (dill) on metabolic
markers in patients with metabolic syndrome; a
randomized double blind controlled trial. DARU Journal of
Pharmaceutical Sciences. 2012; 20(1): 47.

149 S. Jana. G. S. Shekhawat. Anethum graveolens: An Indian
traditional medicinal herb and spice. Pharmacognosy
Review. 2010 Jul-Dec; 4(8): 179–184.

150 Reza Heidarifar. Nahid Mehran. Akram Heidari. Hoda
Ahmari Tehran. Mohammad Koohbor. Mostafa Kazemian
Mansourabad. Effect of Dill (Anethum graveolens) on the
severity of primary dysmenorrhea in compared with
mefenamic acid: A randomized, double-blind trial. Journal
of Research in Medical Sciences 2014 Apr; 19(4): 326–
330.

151 Wahba NM. Ahmed AS. Ebraheim ZZ. Antimicrobial effects
of pepper, parsley, and dill and their roles in the
microbiological quality enhancement of traditional Egyptian
Kareish cheese. Foodborne Pathogens and Disease -
Journals. 2010 Apr;7(4):411-8.

152 Caroline A Gunn. Janet L Weber. Marlena C Kruger. Midlife
women, bone health, vegetables, herbs and fruit study.
The Scarborough Fair study protocol. BMC Public Health.
Jan 10, 2013.

153 Katya P. Svoboda. Janice B. Hampson. Bioactivity of
essential oils of selected temperate aromatic plants:
antibacterial, antioxidant, antiinflammatory and other
related pharmacological activities. Plant Biology
Department, SAC Auchincruive, Ayr, Scotland, UK. 1999.

CARDAMOM
154 Bhattacharjee B. Chatterjee J. Identification of
proapoptopic, anti-inflammatory, anti-proliferative, anti-
invasive and anti-angiogenic targets of essential oils in

Devina H. Collier

cardamom by dual reverse virtual screening and binding pose analysis. Asian Pacific Journal of Cancer Prevention. 2013;14(6):3735-42.

[155] Rena Goldman. Reviewed by Michael Charles, MD. The Health Potential of Cardamom. Healthline.com. July 25, 2016.

[156] Yaghooblou Fatemeh. Fereydoun Siassi. Abbas Rahimi. Fariba Koohdani. Farideh Doostan. Mostafa Qorbani. Gity Sotoudeh. The effect of cardamom supplementation on serum lipids, glycemic indices and blood pressure in overweight and obese pre-diabetic women: a randomized controlled trial. Journal of Diabetes & Metabolic Disorders. September 29, 2017.

[157] Kadiri Sunil Kumar. Aneesha Unnisa. K. Sai Sushmitha. Ashish Lokhande. R. Suthakaran. Antidepressant Activity of Cardamom oil by Marble Burying test in rats. Scholars Research Library. Der Pharmacia Lettre, 2016, 8 (3):279-282.

[158] Paria Azimi. Reza Ghiasvand. Awat Feizi. Behnood Abbasi. Effects of Cinnamon, Cardamom, Saffron, and Ginger Consumption on Markers of Glycemic Control, Lipid Profile, Oxidative Stress, and Inflammation in Type 2 Diabetes Patients. July 2015

[159] Verma SK. Jain V. Katewa SS. Blood pressure lowering, fibrinolysis enhancing and antioxidant activities of cardamom (Elettaria cardamomum). Indian Journal of Biochemistry & Biophysics. 2009 Dec;46(6):503-6.

[160] Gilani AH. Jabeen Q. Khan AU. Shah AJ. Gut modulatory, blood pressure lowering, diuretic and sedative activities of cardamom. Journal of Ethnopharmacology. 2008 Feb 12;115(3):463-72.

[161] Shailee Fotedar. Vikas Fotedar. Cardamom and oral health. Department of Public Health Dentistry, H. P. Government Dental College and Hospital, Shimla, Himachal Pradesh. 2014. Volume 3. Issue 1. Page 86.

[162] Arif ullah Khan. Qaiser Jabeen Khan. Anwar Hassan Gilani. Pharmacological basis for the medicinal use of cardamom in asthma. Bangladesh Journal of Pharmacology. Vol 6, No 1 2011

[163] Pearley Jesylne. Subasree Soundarajan. Karthikeyan Murthykumar. Meenakshi. M. The Role of Cardamom Oil in Oral Health: A Short Review. Research Journal of

Pharmacy and Technology. 2016
164 Archana Sengupta. Archana Sengupta. Cardamom (
Elettaria cardamomum) and Its Active Constituent, I,8-
cineole. Molecular Targets and Therapeutic Uses of Spices,
pp.65-85. May 2009
165 Essential oils used in aromatherapy: A systemic review.
Asian Pacific Journal of Tropical Biomedicine. Volume 5,
Issue 8, August 2015, Pages 601-611.
166 Yaw-Bin Huang. Pao-Chu Wu. Hsiu-Man Ko. Yi-Hung Tsai.
Cardamom oil as a skin permeation enhancer for
indomethacin, piroxicam and diclofenac. International
Journal of Pharmaceutics. Volume 126, Issues 1–2, 29
December 1995, Pages 111-117.
167 Dr. Isaac Eliaz. It's All in Your Gut! How to Enhance Mood,
Immunity and More Through Digestion.
Huffingtonpost.com. March 15, 2012.
168 Das I. Acharya A. Berry DL. Sen S, Williams E. Permaul E.
Sengupta A. Bhattacharya S. Saha T. Antioxidative effects
of the spice cardamom against non-melanoma skin cancer
by modulating nuclear factor erythroid-2-related factor 2
and NF-κB signalling pathways. British Journal of Nutrition.
2012 Sep 28;108(6):984-97.
169 H.Al-Zuhair. B. El-Sayeh H.A. Ameen. H.Al-Shoora.
Pharmacological Studies of Cardamom Oil in Animals.
Pharmacological Research. Volume 34, Issues 1–2, July
1996, Pages 79-82.

GINSENG
170 Ginseng Supplements. WebMD.com. Diet & Weight
Management Reference
171 Lee SH. Lee HJ. Lee YH. Lee BW. Cha BS. Kang ES. Ahn
CW. Park JS. Kim HJ. Lee EY. Lee HC. Korean red ginseng
(Panax ginseng) improves insulin sensitivity in high fat fed
Sprague-Dawley rats. Phytotherapy Research. 2012
Jan;26(1):142-7.
172 Hye-Bin Yeo. Ho-Kyoung Yoon. Heon-Jeong Lee. Seung-
Gul Kang. Ki-Young Jung. Leen Kim. Effects of Korean Red
Ginseng on Cognitive and Motor Function: A Double-blind,
Randomized, Placebo-controlled Trial. Journal of Ginseng
Research. 2012 Apr; 36(2): 190–197.
173 Satish Patel. Nagendra Singh Chauhan. Mayank Thakur.
Vinod Dixit. Hair Growth: Focus on Herbal Therapeutic

Agent. Current Drug Discovery Technologies. June 2015.
174 Hyun-Sun Lee. Mi-Ryung Kim. Yooheon Park. Hyo Jung Park. Un Jae Chang. Sun Young Kim. Hyung Joo Suh. Fermenting Red Ginseng Enhances Its Safety and Efficacy as a Novel Skin Care Anti-Aging Ingredient: In Vitro and Animal Study. Journal of Medicinal Food. 2012 Nov; 15(11): 1015–1023.
175 Mihi Yang. Ho-Sun Lee. Min-Woo Hwang. Mirim Jin. Effects of Korean red ginseng (Panax Ginseng Meyer) on bisphenol A exposure and gynecologic complaints: single blind, randomized clinical trial of efficacy and safety. BMC Complementary and Alternative Medicine. July 25, 2014.
176 Chang Ho Lee. Jong-Hoon Kim. A review on the medicinal potentials of ginseng and ginsenosides on cardiovascular diseases. Journal of Ginseng Research. 2014 Jul; 38(3): 161–166.
177 Dai-Ja Jang. Myeong Soo Lee. Byung-Cheul Shin. Young-Cheoul Lee. Edzard Ernst. Red ginseng for treating erectile dysfunction: a systematic review. British Journal of Clinical Pharmacology. 2008 Oct; 66(4): 444–450.
178 Ik-Hyun Cho. Effects of Panax ginseng in Neurodegenerative Diseases. Journal of Ginseng Research. 2012 Oct; 36(4): 342–353.
179 Soowon Kang. Hyeyoung Min. Ginseng, the 'Immunity Boost': The Effects of Panax ginseng on Immune System. Journal of Ginseng Research. 2012 Oct; 36(4): 354–368.
180 Kyungtaek Im. Jisu Kim. Hyeyoung Min. Ginseng, the natural effectual antiviral: Protective effects of Korean Red Ginseng against viral infection. Journal of Ginseng Research. 2016 Oct; 40(4): 309–314.
181 Jae Gwang Park. Wie-Soo Kang. Kyung Tae Park. Dong Jun Park. Adithan Aravinthan. Jong-Hoon Kim. Jae Youl Cho. Anticancer effect of joboksansam, Korean wild ginseng germinated from bird feces. Journal of Ginseng Research. 2016 Jul; 40(3): 304–308.
182 Jong-Hoon Kim. Cardiovascular Diseases and Panax ginseng: A Review on Molecular Mechanisms and Medical Applications. Journal of Ginseng Research. 2012 Jan; 36(1): 16–26.

Devina H. Collier

Want to Connect?

Get access to wholistic educational nuggets, and online bible studies that you can use for your small group or yourself and loved ones. I hope to chat with you soon!
- DivineNaturalSolutions.com

Want to connect on Facebook?
- Facebook.com/DevinaCollierNaturopath
- Facebook.com/DivineNaturalSolutions

YouTube Channel:
- Youtube.com/c/DevinaCollierNaturopath

Online Herb Store:
- NaturalHealthEdu.com

For speaking engagements, services or other correspondences:
- Info@DivineNaturalSolutions.com
- Divine Natural Solutions (A Private Healthcare Membership Association)
  P.O. Box 515 Flowery Branch, GA 30542

See my other books:
- Hot Flashes, Memory Fog, Mood, and Fatigue
- High Blood Pressure 28 Days Battle Plan
- High Cholesterol 28 Days Battle Plan
- Depression 28 Days Battle Plan
- Anxiety and Stress 28 Days Battle Plan

- Gut Restore 28 Days Battle Plan
- Allergies 28 Days Battle Plan
- Memory and Focus 28 Days Battle Plan

** For the poems, I give special thanks to Ms. Angela Washington from Angelofwords.com. She is an anointed woman of God – a true masterpiece for the glory of God.

Blessing to you and all of yours, Ms. Angela!

www.ingramcontent.com/pod-product-compliance
Lightning Source LLC
Chambersburg PA
CBHW070013110426
42741CB00034B/1228